For Nancy Edwards, Michael Timko, Julian Lamont,
good friends,
and family—

Just because
they intuit and can imagine what is invisible, and
know that a heart can be more than full.

Arlene —
Thank you for your thoughts
sharing your interpretations with
and the class. May your
knowledge base and
happiness continue to
grow.
Regards,
Charlotte

The fire shall ever be burning upon the altar; it shall never go out.

Leviticus, Chapter 6, Verse 13

It is a continual burnt offering, which was ordained in Mount Sinai for a sweet savor, a sacrifice made by fire unto the Lord.

Numbers, Chapter 28, Verse 6

CONTENTS

UNIFYING CLASSICAL IMPRINTS AND CONSTRUCTS IN CULTURE: AN INTRODUCTION

This book has drawn inspiration from both the research and interpretive work of four scholars: Hans Blumenberg (particularly to his *Work on Myth*), Thomas Kuhn (particularly to his *The Structure of Scientific Revolutions* and "The Essential Tension: Tradition and Innovation in Scientific Research"), Angus Fletcher (particularly to his *Allegory: The Theory of a Symbolic Mode* and his most recent *The Color of The Mind: Conjectures on Thinking in Literature*), and Donald Merlin (particularly to his *Origins of the Modern Mind: Three Stages in the Evolution of Culture and Cognition*).

While the nine chapters which compose this text have an interest in some aspects of poetic presentation (poetics), they address both implicitly and explicitly the structural linkages of other texts (divergences and similarities) from the early Greek texts the *Works and Days* and the *Theogony* of Hesiod and more particularly Hesiod's Zeus-Prometheus-Epimetheus-Fire allegory, to the Aeschylean reuse of the Hesiod constructs, and the later British and American proponents of the theme. The book does not propose an interest, per se, in structural semiotics (although they may appear implicitly), but proposes instead an interest in a more fundamental and traditional sense of structure such as is represented by linear and nonlinear repetitions, aspects of framework in areas such as metalinguistics, or skeletal constructions as seen, for instance, in the work of the Russian formal-

1

ists, scholars of myth (both anthropological and literary), the work of the new critics, and within the aegis of critical theory.

As well, however minimally, aspects of the reconstruction, reformulation, retelling, and reinvention of the Hesiod texts present transformations of these texts. Whether or not the transformations or reconstructions surpass the original telling in any kind of transcendental way is entirely dependent upon one's individual sense and interpretation of either personal or formal aesthetics (or both), and the transcendental for that matter. Hesiod's texts, however, no matter how primitively they have been perceived to be, have interests in cognition, the arts, morality, law, politics, psychology, conflict resolution, and a number of other significant issues (including love and aesthetics) which are of the core and body of the history of ideas in literature. The repetitions of these interests and their consequent developments, over time in other works of literature, link aspects of these interests to all disciplines of inquiry—including the humanities, the sciences and the social sciences—as well as to our distant literary, and cultural ancestors. Finally, the ancient Hesiod constructual framework seems to play itself out in the modern period, with minimal repetition in the 1960s and later.

Hesiod, this book proposes, will be seen as an important and paradigmatic generator of much of the cultural past and present particularly in reference to the Zeus-Prometheus-Epimetheus-Fire allegory. Because his structural framework is the construction upon which later authors build, it is acknowledged to be a portentous framework because of the adornments to his texts, and the reconstructions and transformations by later writers who have interests in matters of a literary, scientific, or critical nature which are latent in Hesiod's work and which are symbolically presented by him. Because of historical changes in all areas of human inquiry, however, there are accretions to knowledge which make these transformations of the original paradigm all the more interesting for readers who look at texts from the earliest literary historical epochs. The allegory which is discussed herein is drawn from a gathering of mythic materials. It is the allegory within the myth which draws particular attention because the hidden or latent meanings cannot be discussed completely. As Angus Fletcher has noted in *Colors of the Mind: Conjectures on Thinking in Literature*:

> In literature, perhaps the most obvious carrier of thought is likely to be an allegory of some kind. The ancient Greeks denoted an intellective, cognitive purpose when they called allegory *hyponoia*, or underthought. Allegories could carry meanings hidden beneath the superficial sense of the text. The question that concerns me is: does the thinking process, expressed in an allegory, invoke the concept of literary secrecy, or literary silence? (Fletcher 94)

Perhaps the silence of thought, or notions buried within the silence of this particular allegory, are as provocative as the narratively received and perceived notions which have been part of the public discourse on this topic. For instance, Prometheus has most often been called a "rebel" as if that notion carried some totally satisfactory explication within it. This book hopes to explore more of the associative complexity of the Promethean character, drawing from some interpretive work which has already been produced concerning the fictive Prometheus and his equally fictive forebears. These gods may have something to tell us about ourselves, our potential undermeanings, and interests in our earlier, primordial cognitive strains.

That this allegory is part of a mythic representation only heightens its interest to those interested in allegory and myth. As Donald Merlin notes in his *Origins of the Modern Mind: Three Stages in the Evolution of Culture and Cognition*:

> The social consequences of mythic integration were evident at the cultural level: narratives gave events contextual meaning for individuals. In Paleolithic cultures, and in aboriginal cultures in general, the entire scenario of human life gains its perceived

importance from myth; decisions are influenced by myth: and the place of every object, animal, plant, and social custom is set in myth. Myth governs the collective mind. This remains essentially true today, even in modern postindustrial cultures, at least in the realm of social values. (Merlin 268)

Decoding this allegory within the myths, looking at the open secrets, silent as they may be, is one of the purposes of this book. How authors later reuse these open secrets or undermeanings from the original paradigm make the remnants less secretive and yet voiced in another quiet way—through the aegis of the written word.

1

THOUGHT, JUSTICE AND FIRE, AS SEGMENTS IN CULTURAL, HISTORICAL ALLEGORY— A CASE IN POINT

The narrative of Hesiod's Zeus (translated from the Greek as Thought)–Prometheus (translated from the Greek as Forethought or Foreknowledge)–Epimetheus (translated from the Greek as Afterthought)–Fire allegory is told as a series of stories about the Greek gods and goddesses and of their interactions, at times, with humans. Some aspects of this allegory are sketchily or skeletally presented in Hesiod's texts *The Works and Days* and the *Theogony*. As well, their presentation represents the original paradigm for this particular allegory within literary history. Although these stories are received in what is traditionally called myth, their construct was most clearly identified within an inventory by Angus Fletcher in 1964, in his text *Allegory: The Theory of a Symbolic Mode* and detailed through narrative reuses, not as allegory per se, within various surveys of literature (such as the important *Mysteriously Meant* by Don Cameron Allen in 1970, which details the Medieval and Renaissance reception to earlier redactions of the theme).

Hesiod's stories incorporate the projections of Zeus {Thought} and his cousins, Prometheus {Forethought or Prescient Thought} and Epimetheus {Afterthought} who are brothers within the narrative and separate aspects of thought within mind, in their relationships with one another, to fire, and to humankind. The gods in this book are viewed as human psychic projections, veritable ideas, or ideographs, which correspond to metaphors and other

5

figurative forms of language. Within this book, the characters are viewed on a literal level, as well as the figurative ones, to realize their full importance in as many structural ways as possible.

Hesiod's paradigmatic narrative will be compared with texts which modeled themselves from his construct (eighth-century) through fifth-century Greece (Aeschylus), the British Romantic period (Percy and Mary Shelley), the Victorian period (Charles Kingsley and Robert Bridges), and the Modern period (three portions of books by James Joyce). There will be mentions of aspects of work by Lord George Gordon Byron, James Russell Lowell,—and from the postmodern period—mentions of the work of Robert Lowell and Salman Rushdie concerning the Promethean theme. The Cameron text, noted above, discusses to some extent Medieval and Renaissance hagiographies in his text which relate Prometheus to early Phonecian and Hebrew texts. Although discussions of perceived and recorded Promethean meanings are widely available, several stand out (for instance, *Shelley's Mythmaking* by Harold Bloom and *The Promethean Politics of Milton, Blake, and Shelley*, by Linda Lewis, which briefly discusses Mary Shelley's text *Frankenstein* in an Afterward, and with whom I share agreement concerning several interpretive issues {Frick 1985}). This book attempts to link a large array of British texts out from the Romantics to be compared in relationship to Hesiod's text both implicitly and explicitly, noting changes in ideology from Hesiod's, while keeping an interest in the moral, philosophical, and psychological issues first raised, if but hermeneutically, in his rendering of the Greek gods. Within Hesiod's narrative, the fact that Prometheus gave humankind fire against the express wishes of his cousin, Zeus, is of primary importance to this book figuratively. Fire is perceived by this text to be one of the "open secrets" (Fletcher 94) of Hesiod's allegory which begs for discussion and interpretation. In looking at the figurative importance of fire within the narrative, one must ultimately evaluate the symbolic importance of fire on as many levels as may be thoughtfully perceived. Too, the fact that by going against the wishes of Zeus to keep fire in the pantheon, Prometheus began to reconstruct the nature of "thought" and to deconstruct the central importance of Zeus (a form of monarchical thought). Zeus within the Classical world view, however, was the symbol of the representation of law as well as being the personification and allegorical figure for totality thought. Furthermore, he is the representative of tyrannical thought, and, like a supreme super ego (using the Freudian construct, which will be an interpretive measure within this book), his sense of justice was of primary importance because he was seen as the arbitrator for morality in the early Classical world. Separating Zeus' personal vision from his social vision within Hesiod's narrative is imperative for this book, just as it was an imperative for Prometheus as a character within Hesiod's narrative. Some of Zeus' thought was defined textually by Hesiod as totally destructive to humanity symbolically, and this issue will be discussed in full later in Chapter III. Since Zeus was the representative of the pinnacle of the hierarchy, he was, therefore, the symbolic enemy of humankind at some subjective level to them (within mind or thought) and to other symbolic figures in the pantheon.

Hugh Lloyd-Jones in his *The Justice of Zeus* states of justice in the *Iliad*, an historically resonant work for Hesiod whom has been considered to be Homer's contemporary (although there is no total consensus on this matter), that justice is always concerned with Zeus in his connections with men:

> Zeus in Homer possesses three of the later functions closely associated with that of protecting justice; he is protector of oaths (Horkos), protector of strangers and the law of host and guest (Seinios) and protector of suppliants (Hikesios). (Lloyd-Jones 5)

Also, as given to us in a provocative discourse by Pietro Pucci in his *Hesiod and the Language of Poetry*, justice in Homer is posed by analogy as that which is "straight" in contraposition with that which is "crooked" (injustice). These aspects are allegorized and personified within characters. However, injustice or that which is "crooked" is quite powerful and, although it does not change the nature of justice, it leaves itself open to retaliation (in a personified sense) from justice. Furthermore, it becomes capable of imploding upon itself and, in a metaphoric and personified sense, becomes its own worst enemy (Pucci 45-50). We might compare or suppose, that on this abstract level, this reaction within one's self today to be an analogy to what has been defined as guilt (within being, or consciousness) as part of the incorporation of what was considered "crooked." However, in Hesiod, Pucci continues, justice is pre-Platonic and clearly seems more related to a sense of morality (Pucci 45-50). Thus, by inference, Zeus is both just and unjust—his knowledge of both justice and injustice make him both a good figure and an "evil" or "crooked" one simultaneously; but as the punisher of the "evil" doing and evildoers, his predominant identification would seem to be indicated toward the "good" end of the spectrum, if one could construe such a spectrum.

To note this dual quality of Zeus is to also note its trifocal (synthetic) implication, as well. Based on his knowledge of good and evil, he is persuaded into action, or to a synthesis of positions, as judge of both—which leads to the third position. Also, in Hesiod's *Theogony* and *Works and Days*, Zeus is portrayed as a force of agitation or action which will lead to synthesis. In fact, Zeus often seems to denote the reactive force of nature, whether it would appear as psychic or biological, as extended into human nature, for instance, like a father with an uncontrollable temper. The quality of Zeus's judgment, thus, always seems open to debate. It would seem that Prometheus (his name already defined as forethought, for which he is an allegory), the foil for Zeus, takes up the debate rather well as an act of "humanity" or, more precisely, on behalf of humanity and within thought and mind. For these few reasons, Hesiod's words will help to illuminate the discourse related to this topic. Although Hesiod seems clearly on the side of Zeus in his textual presentations, he makes a presentation of all sides of issues, and particularly those of the two most important allegorical figures, Zeus and Prometheus. Epimetheus, Prometheus' brother, whose name as afterthought, really does seem to be "thrown into" the allegory as an after thought, or upon reflection. But he is also a binary opposite for Prometheus and an important aspect within the process of thought.

Hesiod's rendering of part of the oral tradition, known within literary history as wisdom literature (West 3-26), is useful philosophically because it is both dialectical and didactic, and the rendering implicitly marks his interest in the ideologies which these gods (and symbolic figures of thought) represent. His compilation/fictive history of the genealogy of the gods and stories about them have been documented and translated many times over, insuring the texts' position within the history of literature. In spite of this, some critics underestimate the complexity of Hesiod's paradigm, perhaps because later authors create what seem to be larger dramas than Hesiod's own. M. L. West has spoken well of the scholarly pleasures of Hesiod, for those less inspired to delve:

> I for my part do not presume to tell the reader how much interest there is in Hesiod for him. But I will say that in eighteen years since I began to study this inexhaustible poem in ernest, it has never ceased to disclose something new on each reading; and I do not think any other activity has given me such sustained pleasure and satisfaction as writing about it. (West vii)

No matter what one's individual pleasure in Hesiod, it is appropriate then to acknowledge that later authors out from Hesiod could not have created larger dramas on the topic without Heisod, and, therefore, these early remnants are like fossil records—finds not to be forgotten or ignored. As well, later authors present their individual focus to and from the original which will naturally be divergent from Hesiod's in many, if not most, respects—but the skeletal remnants are clearly there.

Some of the stories of the gods concern their eventual involvements through birthings (also symbolic), and other kinds of interactions with human beings. In the beginning, Hesiod presents Heaven and Earth (the elements and beings of both) clearly linked as our first ancestors through the personification of their characters. Earth was mother to her son Heaven, Ouranos (Wender 15). Her son, Heaven, was father to her other children. On one level, this could be an indication and supposition that human origins have incestuous beginnings. In relation to a reality principle, considering the small number of humans considered to be first alive evolutionarily, the plausibility of this notion is striking.

Apostolos Athanassakis in his *Hesiod: Theogony, Works and Days, Shield* feels, however, that the hegemony of Earth (Gaia) in probability is:

> a remnant from a pre-Indo-European earth-oriented religion in which a ritual castration of the earth goddess' consort signified her supremacy of power and perhaps even corresponded to practice in some aboriginal matriarchal society. (Athanassakis 43)

In Hesiod, however, we are spared knowledge of a first father—as Earth was born after the generation of Chaos, who was not designated with a gender or parental identification. The idea of order being intrinsically linked to chaos is interestingly integral within the paradigm of the new physics of the postmodern era (see *Chaos: Making a New Science* and *Does God Play Dice? The Mathematics of Chaos*). Also reminiscent of the ancient idea in the new physics is the theory that all generation spontaneously sprang from nothing, although what nothing means in this context may need some new definition (Davies 16, 138, 165-166, 195, 199, 201, 203-205, 221). Heinz Pagels in *Perfect Symmetry* has suggested that something comes from nothing when nothing is a curved false vacuum (1992, 340-342).

According to Hesiod's text the *Theogony*, life developed from Chaos whose birth was part of what was considered to be a spontaneous generation, as was Earth's. Why was there no father to Heaven, as a familial pattern had already been established? Perhaps it is a fitting acknowledgement of the strength of Hesiod's texts that origins present the greatest mystery, because the Greeks themselves had determined patrilineal descent. Besides being an indication of an earlier epoch's ignorance of this descent, or knowledge of whom the father might be, it is a rhetorical question related to existence in general—that which was before fathers and mothers, before what is considered to be the corporeal. Hesiod does not go into

any possibilities; they are there for our imaginings. However, his creation presentation has many structural elements in common with creation allegories and myths of
many cultures, as structural studies of both allegory and
myth inform. As well, today we still speculate upon our
origins in physics (as well as in other areas of intellectual inquiry), and of the origins of the universe, as the
after-images of the first (considered to be) spontaneous
generation recorded are being studied (McDonald A8-A10,
and Smoot and Davidson). Yet, the stories of the gods
and humankind in Hesiod's words, words which he tells
us were inspired by the Muses (those illustrious projected
modes of inspiration), concern the destruction and rec-
reation of humankind five times over.

The humans dealt with by Hesiod, whom was an oral
redactor for the community which accepted the ancient
lore, were of the Fifth Age, an age which included himself and which includes ourselves within it; this is the
most corrupted age of all, according to the textual Zeus.
Zeus longed to destroy this Fifth Age, to begin once again.

According to Hesiod, the First Age of personkind, the
Golden Age, is still with us since forms of spirits from
that age live among us, protecting us. But humankind
of the Fifth Age, the Age of Iron, shall be destroyed by
Zeus "when babies are brought forth from the womb with
grey hairs at their temples." Furthermore,

> But, notwithstanding, even these shall have some good
> mingled with their evils. (Evelyn-White 17)

In Hesiod's accounting of justice, according to
Friedreich Solmsen in his book *Hesiod and Aeschylus*:

> Hesiod has fitted these stories into his scheme and
> made them stages in a development which leads be-
> yond them and upwards to the emergence of a more
> human set of gods and a more civilized order of
> things. (Solmsen 25)

As such, Hesiod has brought the gods to their proper
genealogy and species, Homo sapiens. One would assume
on the face of the issue that either the gods were human

or they were gods; but why does Solmsen speak of "a more human set of gods"? Why not "a more human set of humans?" Solmsen leads one to speculate "What is a god?" A god or gods, essentially, within this text will be presented as psychological projections of ideas from the human mind. The psychological projections may be the repositories for inherent communal wishes, hopes, aspirations, descriptions of reality, metalanguage, and language.

Augustine in the *City of God* explicates attitudes related to his response to "gods" and what they represented. He said of the Greeks and their gods:

> It was not, in fact, the men who were preserved by the image, but the image by the men. (Dods 23)

His view of the remains of the iconographic statues of the gods, which were often the size of collectibles, was used by him as his example of his own understanding of these psychologically projected and transferred images. (Aspects of projection and transference will be, then, important methodological and interpretive aspects of this book.) But while reading Virgil's *Aenead*, Augustine formulated one of his arguments in reaction to the collection of idols being sumptuously stolen by the sackers of Troy, in particular, within that narrative.

He sought to compare a "living God," the redemptive Christ, to the images of the "gods" whose forms were realized in stone as statues. They did not conform to known persons, and these loathsome Greek gods were quite unlike Christ, he rationalized, whose very wretchedness (being not living, or capable of love) was their only important iconographic characteristic. His analogy may miss the point, but he posits a way of thinking concerning this issue. The statues of the gods were an attempt to corporealize the ideas (or fantasies) of the gods.

Augustine's understanding is important because his horror at the death and destruction of Troy and the glory, or seeming glory of the victors in stealing from the temples, prevented him from another understanding. First of all, Christianity did not yet exist within that earlier epoch, and the ideas of Christ had not been historically

projected and transferred into the "logos" of world literature. To the Greeks and Romans of another historical
period, the gods and goddesses were part of the status
quo. Augustine's concern was for those individuals who
still believed in gods and goddesses, and for his concern
to help eradicate any remaining belief; he, thus, needed
these arguments of comparison, living as he did historically without the use of modern psychology but clearly
with its implications or underpinnings.

His image for his followers of Christianity was to offer
the image of the personhood of Christ, whom Augustine
felt wholly gave of Himself. This image was to be an ideal
(symbolic and otherwise) for which humankind could
strive in love, or for self-compassion. The gods, however,
were the mass projection of ideas into a space which
seemed beyond the mind, into the cosmos, the great out-
there of the skies. But this place of depiction allows or
allowed the human participant to become involved in an
imaginative interplay with all natural (and fantasy) elements known historically to humankind and to mind, itself, during the era of belief in the pantheon. Augustine
missed the in-built compassion of the fictive Prometheus
entirely as a rational philosophical issue.

Don Cameron Allen tracks some of the recombina-
tions of the early gods and goddesses with figures from
Hebrew and Phonecian texts within his book *Mysteriously
Meant.* Prometheus therein is often deigned to be goodness personified, and other Greek gods are rewritten into
glosses on *Genesis* and within the *Pentatuch.* For instance, Pandora is placed on Noah's ark as one of the
future survivors of the deluge.

Plato, much earlier, was also in reaction against the
gods (and perhaps against Hesiod by inference), in fifth-
and fourth-century B.C. (428-347). He felt that if he could
"do" the world again, in his offerings in *The Republic,* he
would make the gods only "good" and incapable of evil,
quite unlike Homer's portrayal he seemed happy to say:

> The state of the divine must be perfect in every way
> . . .
> for we cannot admit any imperfection in divine good-
> ness or beauty. (MacDonald 73)

This was because Plato felt that wisdom, courage, temperance, and justice would contribute the most good to a commonwealth (MacDonald 73), and these he could not see in the orally depicted traits of the gods of the pantheon. Seemingly these traits, or characteristics, might well be those which the projecting imaginers of "Zeus," or thought, had originally in mind to some degree, but, in Hesiod, Zeus's "temperance" was often an attribute of which he, the fictive character himself, seemed to know nothing. Although temperance was not always considered a valued trait by Zeus, it was considered a valued trait by others dealing with Zeus (because in order to survive the rage of Zeus, temperance was necessary).

The philosopher John Robinson, too, had a reaction to Hesiod's rendering in his book *An Introduction to Early Greek Philosophy*. Robinson stated concerning Hesiod's works:

> Earth and Heaven are not elemental masses in Hesiod; they are persons, and the forces which operate to bring about their separation and reunion are not physical but psychological. In short Hesiod's account of the origin of the world-order is from first to last anthropomorphic. (Robinson 27)

In this statement, Robinson is attempting to separate Hesiod from other early Greek philosophers as being somewhat aberrant and inferior, as Hesiod was considered to be a bard and a story-teller; yet the issues of Hesiod's texts have philosophical relevance. His story of Zeus–Prometheus–Epimetheus-Fire has a philosophy of importance buried within its allegory, and in retelling a story for the people, he is perhaps rendering a people's philosophy which is neither aberrant nor inferior. Hesiod's use of anthropomorphism was the coherent belief of his day, and the vehicle for wisdom; since humans do project their thoughts and fantasies, this use of anthropomorphism does not invalidate Hesiod's own philosophy, albeit his discourse was not similar to that of Anaximander, whom Robinson considers to be the first philosopher. Anaximander's interest in fire (also as a part of the scheme of origins, descriptions, depictions, and analogies) goes something like this:

The heavenly bodies came into being as a ring of fire
. . . The heavenly bodies are wheel-shaped masses of
compassed air filled with fire . . . the sun is like a
chariot wheel . . . the rim of which is hollow and filled
with fire. (28)

Hesiod's own concern was with a beginning, a creation. It, too, was an attempt to explain and understand
the universe. Hesiod considered that he had received his
understanding of this beginning from the gods, who had
been around for sometime in the minds of Greeks (and
stories concerning them) before eighth-century B.C. That
the creation allegory and myth which Hesiod presented
contained cognitive metaphors and allegories which are
still with us today, almost 2,800 years later in varied
forms, testifies to their involvement in what might appear to be a linear, synchronic, and finite construct involved with psychology, philosophy, and the realm of the
physical (as anthropomorphism). Infinity may still baffle
physicists, but provocative, cognitive metaphors seem less
baffling to everyone interested.

To impersonalize the creation, for Robinson, marks
the beginning of philosophy. Some Greeks needed, it
would seem, to personalize the impersonal before they
could make that leap. While at first seeming simplistic
to some degree, personifying Heaven and Earth as the
"creators" of humanity is subtly more abstract and figuratively impersonal than thinking that creation began with
one's own mother and father, and stopping at that point.
Even Charles Darwin's evolutionary theory suggests a
similar truth—perhaps ultimately a greater truth of origins—clearly not told as allegory, although it may be
perceived allegorically within the mind if one perceives
of the iconographical image of humans as apes, and vice-
versa.

A considerable amount of abstraction is evident and
implicit in Hesiod's ordering of the gods and the universe, his rendering. He did not invent the pantheon, but
he inherited the pantheon; although, perhaps he was
inventive in his work (Frick 8). He helped to unify the
already extant stories concerning the gods and life as
perceived in his own time, and before him.

The Prometheus, Epimetheus, and Zeus figures signify the expressions of potentially ambivalent impulses and different kinds of thought, as their names imply. Through the interplay of these allegorical characters, readers can understand their potential as an externalized extrapolation of a psychomachia which could easily be related to intrapsychic conflict and struggle as well, within mind and personality. These issues will be realized and discussed later in the review of the selected Promethean texts.

That Zeus and Prometheus disagreed over what to do with fire is symbolically relevant to the allegory because this impulse (as projected into the beings of gods) allows the interpretative representation of fire not as fire alone, but as an abstraction figuratively, resonant allegorically with potential construed meanings. Using fire as a psychic projection, and to have fire given to those considered unworthy by Zeus (humans, in this case,) is to open its literal meaning to inquiry and figurative exploration.

Infusing "fire" with meaning is to make it anthropomorphically relevant (even personal), at times, through the use of varied "meaning" projections. The meanings for fire may always be in a state of deferral, or flux— just as fire is literally capable of changing into another molecular state and causing changes in other molecular constructs. Since it is almost impossible to rid thought of its corporeal origins within the body, perceiving of fire as a metaphoric construct as well as a literal one, that which is literally not of the body, and then linking it with mind by analogy, or metaphorically (more at the figurative level), allows more of the potential interplay of the structural aspects of fire within the Hesiod texts and, as well, allows its potential deconstructed aspects. Readers can, therefore, see the value of fire and thought as parts of a cognitive symbolic construct in relation to the meanings of the names of Zeus (thought), Prometheus (forethought) and Epimetheus (afterthought). Some scholars (including Linda Lewis and Havelock Ellis) call Prometheus the Forethinker, which he is on one literal level of the narrative, as well as the other aspects which he represents. Which "fire" of the mind will win out, or how will the elements of mind flexibly meld or blend?

Ancient language depicted meanings in ideograms or ideographs, with persons, animals, plants, and social scenarios in relief form "telling the meaning" through the placements of these persons or objects. Donald Merlin in his *Origins of the Modern Mind* describes thoroughly and helpfully the mimetic aspect of language as it evolved from gestures which are considered to be universally similar across cultures. It is clear that Prometheus, Zeus, and Epimetheus do seem to represent three human impulses or intrinsic traits in three separate guises, and fire is an inanimate mediator for them on one level of the narrative. At yet another level, fire symbolically is a metaphor for the mechanism which activates different "kinds of thought," such as those of the characters of the narrative and our own. On another level, it may be seen as a symbol for cognition itself, when all of the segments of thought are fused back together, as when in the realm of physics a black hole forms, collapsing from one molecular reality back into another, taking externally visible light with it.

Furthermore, in suggesting that fire came from "out there somewhere with the gods, from Olympus", delimits the mystery and awesome aspect of not knowing the origins of fire or of man's/woman's ability to think. On a primitive level, therefore, Heisod's explication is structurally useful and sets within literature a beginning construct such as that defined for the sciences by Thomas Kuhn in his text *The Structure of Scientific Revolutions*, wherein accretions to historical scientific revolutions are recognized. As well, the speculative possibility inherent in the projection of these gods (personified, anthropomorphized or allegorized) indicates man's and woman's quest and desire for more knowledge. If one does not know, one often invents an origin or creates a hypothesis to help stave off the anxiety which may come from "not knowing origins."

Hans Blumenberg, the German philosopher, has speculated upon "origins" in a very fascinating way, but more importantly, perhaps, in a very helpful way related to the anxiety of creatures "hominid." Blumenberg, in his *Work on Myth*, asks both himself and his audience in an implicit way, Why do myths survive? He, then, answers that: "A model explanation of such phenomena is in terms of innate ideas" (Blumenberg 151). They survive, he continues, because they represent in Freud's work "the assertion of universal infantile experiences" (Blumenberg 151). Underlying structures of a psychological and cognitive nature are, thus, implied within the mythic texts (the Hesiod texts are both allegorical and mythical) and worth consideration by Blumenberg with just these two examples from Blumenberg; too, these issues were firstly born out within the constructs of Hesiod's allegorical metaphors. In the West, at least, it would seem that

> Homer and Hesiod are our first and, at the same time, most lasting authors of fundamental mythical patterns. (Blumenberg 151)

The fact that these authors of oral origins are from the East (if but the Near East or Mediterranean area) marks part of the cross-culturalism inherent within the origins of Western thought.

DENOTING THE
PROMETHEUS COMPLEX

One need not turn only to Blumenberg to find structural notions and issues related to early human concerns about existence, however, as many mythographers have noted the implicit similar structural constructions of myths which have implications for human behavioral patterns. Myths are paradigmatic and have almost a mathematical certainty about them as well as a decided synchrony in terms of their formulaic expressions for thought and thinking, and constructs for behavior across cultures, as every writer on myth, and anthropologists in the field, have acknowledged. Although Blumenberg's own intellectual forays into myth are more clearly defined and used within the arenas of social and cultural history, with their attendant and necessary impacts on the sciences, at one level, part of his thesis is to prove the "humanist" aspect of the sciences and vice-versa, with what he considers to be the relational scientific aspect of humanism. He uses literary texts to help prove his points, including the mainland European ones related to Prometheus.

Individuals in the sciences, he believes, with their scientific rationality, try to restrict myth to "aesthetic imagination." Romantics in the social sciences and the humanities, including literary theorists, he notes, accept myth as part of "human nature" and as *more important* than "our 'surface' rationality" (Blumenberg vii–viii). He proposes in *Work on Myth* to bridge the gap of what he has perceived as an anti-thesis among these separate realms of inquiry regarding myth. This book, however, is more concerned with what literary writers, and other critical theorists from various disciplines, do with ideas embedded within allegorical/mythical literature, with this particular Hesiod focus, whether the ideas are scientific, humanistic, or a mixture of the two (with the social sciences in for a spin). Hesiod's links to the sciences are evident, if but symbolically evident, as are his links to other areas of what have become human academic inquiry. Much of the groundwork for creative literary authors, early scientists, and social scientists was set by early mythographers and philosophers. Material from the works of Bernard Fontenelle, Pierre Bayle, John Toland, John Trenchard, Richard Blome, William Bosman, Pere Joseph Lafitau, Giambattista Vico, Andrew Ramsay, Samuel Shukford, Ephraim Chambers, Etienne Fourmont, Antoine Banier, Nicolar Frerret, Thomas Blackwell, William Warburton, Noel Antoine Pluche, William Stukeley, Andrew Tooke, Jospeh Spence, Mark Akenside, Robert Lowth, Voltaire, David Hume, Charles De Brosses, Baron D'Holback, Edward Gibbon, Robert Wood, Paul Mallet, James McPherson, Hugh Blair, Christian Gottlob Heyne, Johann Gottfried Herder, Jacob Bryant, Richard Payne Knight, Antoine Pernety, K. P. Moritz, J. W. von Goethe, Sir William Jones, Charles Dupuis, Friedrich Schlegel, F. W. J. Schelling, Friedrich Holderline, Novalis, August Wilhelm Schlegel, and Friedrich Majer has been instrumental if not crucial for the complex development of issues even slightly related to the Promethean theme.

Gaston Bachelard, a French psychoanalyst, from the area of psychiatry and the social sciences, has noted concerning fire this poetic point:

> Le feu est l'ultra-vivant. Le feu ist intime et il est universel. Il vit dans notre coeur. Il vit dans le ciel. Il mont des profondeurs de la substance et s'offre comme un amour. (Bachelard 19)

> (Fire is the ultimate of life. Fire is both intimate and universal. It lives in our hearts. It exists in the heavens. This like the profoundest of substance is offered as love.)

He goes so far as to name, in his connection with fire, "le complexe de Promethee" as the Oedipus complex in

the life of the intellectual or the Oedipus complex of intellectual life, as another metaphor: "le complexe d'Oedipe
de la vie intellectuelle" (27). Bachelard presents his great
intellectual leap, which at first seems so distant from the
celebration of Prometheus as an Attic fire divinity. But
we see that, looking more closely, Bachelard's ideas are
quite in keeping with Greek symbology and allegory. Just
stating the names "Oedipus" and "Prometheus" fill our
minds with images and allusions, if not illusions, without any more descriptive language—particularly if one is
familiar with any of these texts.

No one, though, elevated the fire-carrier Prometheus
higher in the imagination of intellectuals and within literary aesthetics than Aeschylus who was the first to dra-
matize Prometheus within literary history after Hesiod.
On the physical level, Aeschylus had Prometheus bound
to a mountain top in his play, before his audience. By
concentrating linguistically upon Hesiod's brief aural
images concerning this allegory, making them visual, and
by accepting them, Aeschylus both shows to us and expands Prometheus' symbolic power. It is this symbolic
power of Prometheus in the minds of readers and audiences which is significant—because with Prometheus
comes the gift of fire from "Olympus," that symbolical
nowhere or somewhere (other than that literal designated
site in Greece), if it can only be located within the minds
of readers and literary historicists through imagination.

Prometheus had so angered another god, within both
of Hesiod's texts, that a great revenge was concocted for
him, and Aeschylus' fascination with the punishment is
played to the maximum for his audiences. Yet, within
Aeschylean dramatic irony, the elevation and exposure
on the mountaintop is also the signification of
Prometheus' temporary impotence, which Aeschylus uses
to his own advantage as author for the purposes of his
own explication of the Promethean dilemma. Is it that
guilt and punishment may be the accompaniments of
great insight and efforts to contribute to the potential
constructive behavior of others, and to society in general, he seems to be rhetorically asking. Major setbacks,
it is implied, may be in order for those who take risks,
or contradict the "truth" or thought of another in higher
authority, even if the thought of the "highest" authority

is in contradiction to internally, both for the individual and society, more constructive recognitions. Intrapsychically, forethought (or thinking for tomorrow and the survival of one's self and others) may pose the reality or need for psychological readiness and the struggles against potential guilt and/or punishment problems which may be attendant thereupon or therewith. Prometheus' binding to a rock partakes, then, of oxymoronic principles. Although he was victorious ultimately in more ways than in one, he paid a price for his victory.

Aeschylus took the early Hesiod images and the idea of Prometheus so seriously that this image of the seeming martyrdom of Prometheus is still potent. This god within literary history, is unbound by both Percy and Mary Shelley within the Romantic landscape, and by other authors of the Victorian period. However, in one postmodern text, Salman Rushdie's text *Grimus* (considered to be science fiction), the remnants of Prometheus (and thus semiotically of his two relatives) are transformed within the paradigm of postmodern physics. Rushdie uses the image of a narrative collapse of reality as a seeming metaphoric black hole (which is more like a worm hole within a black hole), wherein the mass of one everyday life reality is transformed into another. As well, within his text he unites standardly accepted Western themes, including Prometheus, with more Eastern ones.

This allegory has then been embodied within the corpus of literature at different literary junctures, and our interpretations are clearly a projection of mind and aspects of cognition to be interpreted and reinterpreted, just as the literary texts themselves may be. For Prometheus, as a character, both created and loved as we do, and what becomes of Hesiod's allegory, finally, reveals much about literary historical preference and progress. Zeus is gradually replaced or absorbed into, and by, a literary and historical authorial preference for the Prometheus suit met with a new kind of force, the authorial one—the new kind of prescient "thinking being" described within the allegory as forethought, or one who is prepared for positive action for the potential of a tomorrow. Aeschylus gives to readers a god who cares for humans:

The miseries of men
I will recount you, how, mere babes before,
With reason I endowed them and with mind;
And not in their disparagement I speak,
But of my gifts to memorize the love:
Who firstly seeking, knew not what they saw,
And hearing did not hear; confusedly passed
Their life-days, lingeringly, like shapes in dreams,
Without an aim; and neither sunward homes,
Brickwoven, nor skill of carpentry, they knew;
. . .
Of healing drugs they wasted, till that I
Showed them to mix each virtuous remedy,
Wherewith they shield them now from all disease.
. . .
Nay, take the whole truth briefly, in a word,
All skill that mortals have, Prometheus gave.
(Whitelaw 14 [see Murray])

This huge embodiment of power in one allegorical idea, or one character, as being, is a capitulation of everything which Zeus, god of gods, stood for ideologically within Hesiod. Aeschylus' transformation of Prometheus from a thief to a giver of multidimensional life bears the suggestion of Prometheus as a projection of an idea of collective artisans, an indication of humankind's creative drive and desire for survival rendered symbolically.

The collective sensibility was the very thing in Hesiod's texts which flayed Zeus's imaginings and power as allegorical representation of "thought" undelineated into "kinds" of thought, in his fear or hatred of mankind/womankind. This rigid notion of the fixed "thought", too, could be a symbolic projection intrapsychically of potential aspects of masochism, or self-destructive impulses. However, this "fixed" notion of "thought" implanted within one being is tyranny as we have come to define it within government or even within one psyche, in Freudian terms, as a rigid super ego drive. This fixed aspect to the characterization of Zeus represents his "Achilles' heel", or the Achilles' heel to this kind of totality thinking. That Prometheus may have represented a wish for too collective a kind of force, ultimately, may have been his Achilles' heel symbolically, extra-textually, and intertextually. Perhaps he was just the wish (or possibly the collective forethought) for a more constructive life. Intrapsychically, however, forethought still exists. Whether microcosmically expressed, however, in psychological forms, or macrocosmically, in nature and government, the emotions toward collective idealizations or hierarchic ones in excess in either direction would probably undermine any psyche, government, or system of belief as seen in too tyrannical capitalistic forms or too tyrannically imposed communal ones. One without the other element would represent a stagnant pool wherein conflict and confluence adding to the necessary change would be absent, dangerously absent. The fact that Zeus could not tolerate difference from his own thought, which ought to have been able to accommodate both forethought and afterthought within it, is an indication of the psychological and philosophical problems discussed through the political characterizations of the ideas within the narrative of the allegory.

The belief, per se, in the pantheon had to diminish historically. This interest diminishment or self-destruct mode seems to be a built-in aspect of the lines of the narrative itself, primarily of Hesiod's work, and how this happens will be shown. Both the glory and complexity of the pantheon still exist thematically as the pantheon has been re-created in various metaphoric forms with various meanings historically; and postmodern authors still play with the theme and the allegory in renderings of neoClassical forms, and even more modern abstracted ones. Our individual beliefs have taken other forms; but some of these beliefs are still analogous symbolically with Classical ones structurally and thematically. For instance, light and fire are extrinsically and intrinsically important to Judaic and Christian thought, both literally and figuratively. As well, they are important within the paradigms of postmodern physics and cosmology wherein scientists are beginning to define chaos and creation, and within other areas of the sciences in general.

Although it may seem like a truism, which does not necessarily diminish its truth value, readers cannot forget the necessary symbology involved within the invention of the gods because in understanding the remnants, or seemingly more important elements, we may understand our cultural history more clearly and definitively, if but allegorically presented and allegorically perceived. The ever longing, loving need to tell a story is still with us as is our ever longing, loving need to share knowledge in all its disparate forms. However, the *re-creation* or transformation of Hesiod's original allegory is telling in and of itself, although it is clearly not the only ancient story which has been retold in various forms; it is one of the most important, nevertheless.

In *Thieves of Fire*, Denis Donoghue, the literary historicist and critic, suggests that:

> My interest in the transmission of the Promethean myth is incidental to another interest, that of recognizing the hero in the imagination of certain writers who may or may not claim him directly. I am interested in describing a certain kind of imagination as Promethean. Let us assume that we are in a world dear to Stevens, where men having taken the place of gods and demigods, think their own imagination divine, with consequences not yet exhausted. . . . We are concerned with imaginations which, in one degree or another have taken the place of Prometheus. If we have seen Prometheus dispelled in mid-air, we have also seen his spirit in the imagination of certain writers, and the proof is in their style, their way of addressing themselves to reality . . . (Donoghue 34)

It is in this kind of spirit, which Donoghue so aptly describes, in its direction, that many of the ideas in this book will continue to lead and develop. Like Hesiod, Professor Donoghue strives for an understanding of a "more civilized order of things" to use Solmsen's words. (Harold Bloom also acknowledged, but not descriptively or symbolically, that Prometheus, as a construct, was a part of all of our psyches in his *Shelley's Mythmaking* {Bloom 106}). There is something civil, in the best sense of the meaning of the word, in the presentations and transformations of the allegory. Artists, humanists, scientists, social scientists, and varied professionals (in all strivings) are decreed the symbolic spirit of fire and the literal care of fire when this is possible as a birthright, with all the attendant positive and urgent responsibilities of this inheritance.

Dr. Alfonsina Albini Grimaldi states in her book *The Universal Humanity of Giambattista Vico* that:

> It is to this god within himself, to the various manifestations of his inherent power that man has raised altars and worshiped as his benefactor. For instance in Apollo he adored his own adeptness in the art of medicine, in Mercury his eloquence, in Orpheus his gift for creating harmony. (Grimaldi 96)

In Prometheus, we find the recognition of the need for self love, but of a self love which is not separate from vanity, but which in itself is not all vanity. The recognition is of the need to fight both the sense and reality of oppressive forces, from within the psyche or externally, which try to still self-expression, self-value, self-meaning and self-knowledge through which we experience knowledge of life and others with all of the implied and real versatility inherent within cross-cultural "anotherness." If one looks into a clear pool and does not recognize the image of one's self, if the mirror of the soul does not shine forth in recognition, all is vanity (as the book of *Ecclesiastes* informs, and as Herman Melville has renoted in *Moby Dick*) and all is lost, for like Narcissus, that powerful embodiment of the lack of self-knowledge, one shall drown in one's own ignorance and negative infantile stubbornness.

One of the very strong signifiers inherent in the Zeus-Prometheus-Epimetheus-Fire paradigm is that Zeus, Prometheus, and Epimetheus are the physical representations of a dialectical struggle. In the most societal way, their struggle is expressed as that between civil democrats who are linked to a seeming monarchical, immovable force, in a struggle not for revolution, it would seem, but for systematic, humanistic change in a world which has often been defined by its fears and interest in self-destruction, much as Sigmund Freud describes in his *Civilization and Its Discontents*. As such, the driving idea behind this particular allegory is that of a psychic projection of a basic understanding of the need for a systematic approach to survival wherein different kinds of thought are accepted by the general population by an indulgence in and dialogue with this didactic literature (and others like it) both presented and reused by later authors. It is their reader-writer responses, and the audience indulgence of these themes, and participation with these themes, which ultimately *allow* the projection of the inherent ideas of the texts, although they may be rewritten or reinterpreted by other authors within cultural and literary history for the subjective and objective needs of the particular period which the author represents.

In the nineteenth-century, there is a Classical collision with themes and thoughts of science, wherein the ideas of Prometheus are joined to those of Darwin, most notably within a literary text for children and adults of all ages called *The Water Babies*, which is described in a later chapter. After this collision, Prometheus will never be quite the same kind of figure again, nor will either the hero or heroine of literature be quite the same again. It is because of Darwin and the incorporation of his paradigm into popular culture and the literary corpus that we collectively find our metaphorical and symbolic "earthy" libido, which we could not have understood so clearly before.

As one allows responses to the allegory, one sees the structural implications of many modern thoughts buried within the "action" or semiotics of the narratives. Acknowledging this, one can then approach the possibilities for interpreting the structural similarities across texts historically. The civil democrat, Prometheus, indulges in a kind of "civil obedience" (not disobedience) to his inward, strong and good consciousness. The monarchical republican, Zeus, as king of the gods, so to speak, or god of gods, does not react well to this at first, but his later authors rewrite him, not surprisingly. Hesiod's Zeus is seen, as well as the representative of nature's imminence over all, as the one who wished to destroy the human population of the earth. Prometheus challenges what he sees as a destructive impulse in his cousin, and interacts on behalf of humankind not out of a need for defiance, although it might seem so and be interpreted so, but out of what Aeschylus termed and expressed as necessity. Perhaps it is a necessity within mind, allegorically (that is, symbolically), to struggle over issues, reviewing different thoughts before coming to fixed thought which itself (that final fixed thought) has the potential to explode or transform into something other, as fire originates and dies, as another formulation.

Narratively, Prometheus cannot fool Zeus about his interactions with humans because these gods were born, if but fictively, equals in wit; this was a part of the birthright of each. Zeus eventually tries (tries because he is not finally successful) to punish Prometheus, the primary reason being for Prometheus' act of giving fire to humankind, or perhaps more importantly allegorically, for acknowledging and struggling for various forms of thought instead of one fixed mode. But, in the meantime, Zeus himself, narratively in Hesiod at least, becomes more involved with humans, and, therefore, within mind.

In Aeschylus' text, Zeus will allow the release of Prometheus after one of his own descendants (conceived with Io, herself human) bears a child, a black child, most interestingly named Epaphos or Touchborn, who will be the first of thirteen generations (Scully 67 or Whitelaw 23) removed from Io, eventually to culminate in the birth of Heracles or Hercules, the liberator of Prometheus. Heracles is the culmination of a liberation which might be emulated because of the nondiscriminatory aspects implied within ancestry. Indeed, some postmodern geneticists and social scientists determine that humanity's common ancestry is African, the divergent cultures of which are now a blend of diverse cultures.

The resolutions to the struggle between cousins is a metaphoric message which signals the "birth" of rule by reason over brute force, expressing the need for reason but also for compassion in an otherwise seemingly chaotic universe. The struggle is concerned with the power of ideologies: Zeus defined as destructive—because of his potentially death directive ends—and Prometheus as constructive because of his willingness to make a gift of fire, in terms of both literal and figurative survival; his kind of thought is ours to have. Although it is ultimately the Promethean ideology which survives most intact, it does not survive without the change of consent of its original antithetical obstacle, Zeus. In this sense, the varied forms of cognition and ideation (through the melding fire) are survivors and contributors to a better, and strongly linked, understanding. This understanding and "its action" are unfolded in Chapter III.

It is often difficult to be fully conscious of the metaphoric content of Hesiod's stories, partially because of the nature of the narrative. One slips in and out of the story line in the telling, and one is not smacked full force with polemic or "truth" and philosophy. However, because of the suspension of time and belief (far away from Hesiod's time and belief), and because of our own historical identifications and their often "quasi" status within our own individual psyches, relevant insights, creative interpretations, and re-creations other than the original literal story lines have survived. However, one is nonetheless drawn back to the metaphoric content and element of Hesiod because his personal voice is a powerful undercurrent in the iconographic ideograms of the narrative or of the semiotic implications within the construction of the narrative and its derivatives. His original desire in his own lifetime was to both reprimand morally and to help his brother Perses learn to grow intellectually and emotionally, and to expound to the kings and the audiences of his day. His narrative has been expanded to these outer limits, hundreds of years hence; he could not have perceived of this historicism, ultimately. Linda Lewis presents a collection of dramatic relevant drawings, paintings, and prints concerning some of the iconographic remnants of the theme and its relevance to Christian thought and extant iconography in her excellent and thorough text *The Promethean Politics of Milton, Blake, and Shelley.*

The anthropomorphic "play" of characterization, place, time, and action of the Hesiod allegory is not always playfully told, as there is much violence within the interplay of his presented elements. As well, Hesiod's paradigm is the original recorded construct of the telling of the gods (because we do not know the other oral poets who participated in the transmission of the narratives) in a theogony; as such, its religious value has not been underestimated historically. How this construct is used historically, through literature and other cultural ways in a fictive manner, places the theme in a finite/

infinite paradoxical possibility within our minds and literature in terms of meaning. If we believe in the ultimate deferral of meaning—perhaps there will be no absolute finite meaning to this allegory. But because of the allegory's representation within time, in its various forms, the allegorical construct seems to eliminate diachronic "time" paradoxically, seemingly, as a final construct for consideration as the allegory seems to fall more heavily into an arena of received synchronic meaning, which allows for varied interpretations and playfulnesses for assertive readers, writers, and audiences to the texts (however the texts may be presented and in whichever literary epoch). One is kept in touch with the distant past through our interpretations, making that past seem less strange ultimately, less far within time, and less diminished both emotionally and intellectually. In quantum reality, since the exposition of Albert Einstein's general theory of relativity, Werner Heisenberg's uncertainty relations, Max Born's indeterminacy, Niels Bohr's complementary concepts, Stephen Hawking's black hole equations, and George Smoot's discovery of the afterimages of creation (Smoot and Davidson), time will never be considered the same "time" that it once was (Pagels 78-109 and 295). Today, even thought and intelligence are speculated to be a part of an internal quantum reality, with invisible and mysterious aspects yet to be understood (Chopra 107 and 217). This ancient and retold allegory has been an attempt to intuit and to imagine the invisible process of thought.

The name of Prometheus has been born through the ages, to be reborn in various texts (including musical ones), and fantasy. Although it may seem impossible to leap 2,300 years from Aeschylus to Mary Shelley's Promethean text (*Frankenstein, A Modern Prometheus*), a surprising continuity of symbols are retained, even if used for different cognitive ends. The remnants of the paradigm are still solidly vital and meaningful, in varied ways, all those many years later. The structural similarities are remarkable, and by analogy and metaphor within her text (see Chapter IV), they will be linked ever more closely to the original.

CONSIDERATIONS WITHIN HESIOD AND AESCHYLUS

Hesiod's epistemology (his theory of the nature and grounds of knowledge) and ontology (nature of being) in eighth-century Greece were his incorporated expressions of the gods and goddesses into the literary corpus of his day. And, according to Hesiod:

> they taught Hesiod glorious song . . . and breathed into me a divine voice to celebrate things that shall be and things that were aforetime; and they bade me sing of the race of the blessed gods that are eternally, . . . (Evelyn-White 79-80)

He knew, even then, that things "would" come from his rendering. The gods are the ideas, the song, and basically represent the soul of the matter, philosophically, for they were also their own inspiration, a priori, it would seem, before they could be Hesiod's. Hesiod, thus, partakes of Prometheus (forethought), a conduit for that which existed before time, and exists beyond time. Hesiod's metaphysics are inherent in the telling of the births of the primary gods and goddesses, and of their own children, and his belief in his own words, his song. We learn from Hesiod of the many wonders of his universe, and within his pantheon, late into the text, of Zeus and Prometheus (primarily), two of those wonders whose relationship acts as a bulwark for larger issues, not known to them within the narrative line as they are partially protected from their own allegorical intents and aspects of their own ancestral prehistory (such as one primordial castration, various god denouements, and foretold and continuous birthings). The story of Zeus–Prometheus–Epimetheus (kinds of thought) is a foreshadowing of the denouement of the pantheon, itself, in the sense that their (the characters as forms of thought) particular section of the tale entails and encompasses contact with humankind—for both good and ill, for all time. The god and goddess "contact" is kept alive by incorporation into mind and within literary history through continued reading, writing, and explication of Classical texts. Hesiod's narratives are myriad with meanings, some of which we may never know or intuit. They are intense just on the literal story line. But a sketch of the Hesiod *Theogony* shows the reader how Zeus, as the third king of the gods, was an improvement over his ancestors. Also, the brief description which will follow will also link us, again, to themes of life and death taken up so forcefully and convincingly within Ernest Becker's postmodern text *The Denial of Death.* For one aspect of Prometheus (forethought) is that he has extraordinary power over Zeus; he has eternal life, he knows the time of Zeus' denouement, and can save him from this denouement if freed to do so. Thus, on the symbolic level of the narrative, would the ego save the needed aspects of super-ego. Prometheus does not have to deny death, as his is a represented form of wisdom that goes beyond death. Zeus on the other hand, feared death (his demise) and wished to obviate it.

As a synopsis, the first of Hesiod's gods was Heaven, who Cronos castrated with the help of his mother Earth. Earth was angry with Heaven because Heaven hated many of his own children; he especially hated the Cyclops, the orb-eyed, and those children of the one-hundred-hands, which were so grotesque to him. (This first castration, reminds postmoderns of Freud's hypothesis in *Totem and Taboo* of the ritual murder of the first father.) These children were considered to be deformed by Heaven and he was afraid of them. They had to be hidden in caves beneath the earth, or within it. This form of scapegoating, though seemingly more subtle today, has always been a consideration for a ritualized way of purging the fearful person of real, imagined, or only feared intrapsychic faults (see Robert Burn's *The World of Hesiod, A Study of the Greek Middle Ages, c. 900-700*). Hesiod boldly announced that this kind of antagonism is a form of jealousy on the part of Heaven:

> He was jealous of their exceeding manhood and come-liness of size. (125)

Cronos, rightly or wrongly considering the act itself, decided to help his mother Earth to forcefully deprive Heaven of his strength through castration, perhaps a symbolic one only. Earth represents the posture of allowing all forms of humanity to experience, or metaphorically, to the light of day. She wants her children, all of them, restored from their places of banishment, usually under the earth or within it.

Cronos, later, upon becoming king of the gods, himself, had his own fears of his children. It was foretold that he would be supplanted by one of his children, and this ought to have been just accepted, perhaps, as *the due right of inheritance* to one of his children; however, Cronos began to swallow the children, one by one, on the date of birth. His behavior replicates that of Heaven in the sense that it is a form of denial, and not necessarily to the prophecy of his replacement, itself. In its primitive form, the swallowing, as the hiding in the caves, may represent an attempt at a denial of death, or a denial of the competitive spirit that the children have naturally come to represent. The swallowing is also a denial of emotions, then, on the figurative level. It could also be a denial of the fantasy of a feared loss of potency—or one explanation of the figurative implication. Zeus, miraculously it would seem, was spared from the ritual "swallowing" routine of his father through the conspiracy and connivance of Heaven, Earth, and Rhea (Cronos' sister/wife). So, even though Heaven had been earlier castrated, or stopped from his bad behavior, he was not finally considered to be an impotent figure. In some sense, he was restored to the community; he was still capable of action. As he was the foreteller of Cronos' fall, having experienced his own fall once, he has a proper credible voice: the statistical evidence is his. Bad or "crooked" behavior does not pay for any length of time—as the narrative seems to indicate—although like evil, it looks as if it does upon occasion.

However, Zeus, at the appropriate experiential juncture in his life, showing a certain inevitability of form, precedence, and rights of passage, then enjoined with many Titans and children of Titans to fight Cronos. Cronos was forced to "throw up his children" at this point, and Zeus was later awarded lightning and thunder by his "monstrous" uncles after he had unbound them from the wraps of Cronos. (This binding/unbinding motif marks a prefigurement and a precedent for the binding/unbinding of Prometheus, although he was just a cousin, not a son, uncle, or brother of Zeus). A great battle ensued at the unbinding, in which Cronos was forced into Tartarus (a place described as beneath the earth, which would take a year's traveling time to reach, or a dropped anvil falling nine days through space, reaching its final destination at the end of the ninth day). This motif is familiar to Satan's fall within John Milton's *Paradise Lost*, as noted by other scholars.

Furthermore, Hesiod continues to implicate the pantheon in internecine, familial conflict by naming Iapetus, though he plays no significant role in the conflict itself, as the brother to Cronos, uncle to almighty Zeus, and *father* to Prometheus. Iapetus, then, was a Titan, (not Prometheus in Hesiod), along with Cronos, a relevant point which is often confused or overlooked. Iapetus had three other important sons. One was Atlas, who held the sky upon his back; interestingly, Zeus fathered a child with Atlas' daughter Maia—and this child was Hermes. Another of Iapetus' important children was Epimetheus, or afterthought, (who is always in jeopardy of being left out of the allegory altogether, unless one gets the afterthought to remember him). He had an important marriage to Pandora. Pandora was a golem, or something like one, it would seem, who was actually created by

Hephaestus, the "limping" god. Structurally, Hephaestus was born as an analogous birth to Athena. (He was born without love by Hera, just as Athena was born without love [but perhaps fictive self love] through her father).

Monetius, another brother to Prometheus, was killed by Zeus for what Zeus deigned to be excessive arrogance, though Hesiod does not indulge readers with any details concerning this presumed arrogance. Zeus, however, understands excesses, and is begging to be controlled. His understanding of Monetius may have been a projection of his own excesses, which he himself denied and did not understand, except as he perceived excesses in and through others.

Within Hesiod's work, it is most expediently stated that Zeus and Prometheus, cousins (first cousins at that), were, according to Zeus, equals in wit. We shall see that in other ways Prometheus preceded or exceeded Zeus in insight and projection of insight (as his name may imply). This does not mean that Prometheus was superior to Zeus. Neither does it indicate inferiority. Importantly, two other cousins of Prometheus, second cousins, Hephaestus and Hermes have often been named in relation to fire.

The *Homeric Hymns*, a collection of rhapsodies, considered to have their origination in the fourth-century by imitators of Homer, and clearly of Hesiod, name Hermes not only as messenger of the gods and tender of cattle, but also as the *inventor* of fire. (So the literary word goes out from Hesiod and Homer, and changes, or gets reimagined). Hephaestus, the mighty one skilled in crafts and metal work, is also named therein as a fire god. Both play important roles in Aeschylus' *Prometheus Bound*. Hephaestus was the unwilling binder of Prometheus and Hermes, acting as a henchman for Zeus, antagonized Prometheus after his binding in that Aeschylean tragedy. *The Homeric Hymns* begin to show how a good idea takes off in the imaginations of artists/writers, becoming more embellished, complex, yet linked to origins.

Back in the eighth-century, associations had been further complicated by Hesiod's own embellishment upon a theme, his own (or those who claim him) theme at that.

In his *Catalogues of Women and Eoiae*, wherein Hesiod named Deucalion as a son of Prometheus, Deucalion has a daughter named, yet again, Pandora. Zeus, in imitation of Epimetheus to some degree, whom he fooled with his golem creation, fathers a child with a Pandora, and this child, Graecus, could be considered symbolically as the forerunner of the Greek polis, or the linking of the monarchic republic, potentially a tyranny, with its more democratic potential.

Furthermore, although Zeus may be seen sexually as an archetype for the decadent Don Juan character as he evolved culturally and in literary history, in Hesiod's intent, it would appear that Zeus is not meant to be negatively configured. The Zeus reign eventually became ameliorative to the Prometheus' impulse, and to the idea of the more stable elements of personhood. Zeus and Io through the help of one of their descendants (Hercules) liberate Prometheus or forethought, incorporating him allegorically into Zeus's own thought pattern, and vice-versa. Hesiod has given his readers a construct which shows behavioral change over time, a symbolic contribution to ideas, expressed through allegory, of the potential variety of kinds of thought within mind, culture, and literary history.

Giambattista Vico felt that

> Fear of the superior force they imagined expressing
> its wrath in the thunderbolt and the flash of light-
> ning (Grimaldi 96)

brought rude, primordial men and women "within the pale of civilization." In that sense, one might suggest that we are probably all rude and primordial, to some degree, not because of the wrath we imagine to be inherent in the thunderbolt and lightning, but because of our awareness of the reality of their capability to destroy our lives and to damage our very corporeal bodies. Vico was correct for everyone in this depiction. But just as interestingly, Vico was convinced that the wisdom of these rude, primordial people, or much of it, has for centuries lain buried within the etymology of their words. One can take for examples of this wisdom the names of Zeus,

Prometheus, and Epimetheus. The ideas expressed within their names encourage complex reflection for meaning. Often the meaning seems extrinsic to the narrative line, or as one of its open secrets.

The important linkage of their names is an attempt to postulate and describe differences or purposes of various kinds of thought and the indication of discriminations among types of thought and cognition, or cognitive awareness. Zeus, for instance, the monolith, makes arbitrary judgments and has ambivalence about many of the actions which he takes. Zeus within Hesiod is seen as thought unchecked, full force, in all its effusive and potentially diluted and deluded stages. He differed from his father and grandfather in the respect that he *did* elevate some of his children—there was progress in his reign. However, within his autocracy, he was the maker of moral judgments and he himself was a womanizer, indulging in an actively promiscuous life, not all without a cumulative rationale, however. Many of his liaisons had ameliorative outcomes and positive political ones, in the final analysis, if that justifies his evolution by noting that.

Prometheus' thought represents, rather, a form of premeditated thought; his representation is as a selective, conscious evaluator and actor. He stands for mortals and/or the self no matter how or what the seeming consequences. He seems to embody the ethical mind, even though Hesiod calls him a "trickster." (In indigenous American literary lore, the trickster has been interpreted by Paul Radin as the representation of the id force within society.) For Hesiod, however, Prometheus was making something of a fool of Zeus, something which he did not like ultimately and he notes this emotion in his text. Epimetheus in Hesiod's narrative is portrayed as somewhat unintelligent and dim-witted. Epimetheus was warned by Prometheus not to take a gift from Zeus, whom he feels is a trickster. But as an afterthought to this warning, he does take a gift from Zeus—the gift of Pandora. Epimetheus even marries her. Pandora is more than a gift of Zeus; she is also his creation, formed from earth and water, bedecked, as well, with beauty by various other gods and goddesses, meant to seduce and destroy resistance.

Pucci in his chapter on Pandora in *Hesiod and the Language of Poetry* describes her as an ambivalent gift, based on her creation and the nature which she was meant to imbue through her formation. Pandora supposedly let all evil loose in the world, and saved only hope in her jar. And, yet, the reader is aware that all evil was already loose in the world, as witnessed in Zeus' seeming unmitigated behavior. The jar can be seen as a shibboleth, or displacement, of the actual evil, which made woman look possibly like the cause and guilt bearer of universal wrongs, although she was not and is not. However, for Epimetheus to accept what is or was, all of evil already loose in the world, was not quite so dim-witted as it may have seemed, but the acceptance of a reality principle. Pandora was just the metaphoric "other" —and scapegoat—who symbolically held the resonance of what was already available in the world. Her "hope" completes the exposition of the ambivalence which Pucci discusses, perhaps its most positive aspect. If ever so ironic, Zeus's union with his other Pandora, Deucalian's daughter, seems to be a unifying principle, the act of one in the logos, as the mirror resonance of hope. This occurrence indicates unifying activity not only on a physical level but on political and emotional grounds as well. Ethics within the text, because of this union, seem more balanced, whether or not the union also indicated evidence of social and gender balance. It is clear that the golem Pandora did not have a mind of her own, but was, as a totemic figure, a convenient "imitation of woman" upon which to place the burden of evil.

The paradigm of the archetype of Zeus-Prometheus-Epimetheus, and their mighty fire, is structurally constructed and told quite sparingly in both the *Theogony* and the *Works and Days*. It is first mentioned in the *Theogony* in the chronology of Iapetus' sons:

> And ready-witted Prometheus, he bound with inextricable bonds, cruel chains, and drove a shaft through his middle, and set on him a long-winged eagle, which used to eat his immortal liver; but by night the liver grew as much again everyway as the long-winged bird devoured in the whole of the day. (Evelyn-White 17)

It was because of an earlier "crime" of Prometheus that Zeus had decided to keep fire from the human race, although this withholding could be a fictive narrative excuse, or displacement, for his anti-human sentiments. However, at Mecone, at a feast of gods and "mortal men", Prometheus gave men ox flesh to eat, but gave Zeus only the fat and bones of the ox to eat, in such a carefully disguised manner which made Zeus' portion look the best. This was provocative of Prometheus, and perhaps unnecessary. However, it was both a literal and figurative indication of his underlying preference for the human, and an exposition of imagination as a potent, synthetic tool. Then after Prometheus gave humans fire, Zeus enchained him and had the limping god (Hephaestus) create Pandora in revenge, or what seemed revenge to Zeus at the time. In this punishment, it must be noted that the creative spirit, the giving spirit (of Prometheus) is regenerative and indestructible, just like his almighty liver. In analogy, Prometheus is like Freud's id energy from which ego and libido are derived, and which deflates the superego (Zeus), to help support the ego (its positive elements) of both the individual and humanity, as a mirror image, extending outward from himself. Epimetheus could be equated to what is now called, symbolically, libido because of his marriage to Pandora, which in some ways may be seen as an ameliorative act, in spite of the complete interplay, both negative and positive, of the loaded jar imagery.

In the *Works and Days*, Hesiod mentions that Zeus hid fire from humans because Prometheus had deceived him—but Hesiod does not mention the deception therein, and we are left to wonder if it is a reference to the ox meat incident mentioned earlier. In the *Theogony*, Hesiod stated of Zeus:

> therefore he planned sorrow and mischief against men.
> He hid fire; but that the noble son of Iapetus stole
> again for men from Zeus the consellor (sic) in a hollow fennel-stalk . . . (5-6)

What Aeschylus does with this skeletal framework is truly monumental, both literally and figuratively, for the greatest detail of what happens to Prometheus is developed within the *Prometheus Bound*. For Aeschylus this punishment for presumed guilt is something rather extraordinary because Prometheus was helping the *other*, the symbolic ego of mankind, not himself, on most levels. His was a seemingly selfless act, although symbolically it is an indication of a confident ego; he disagreed that humankind ought to be destroyed, and that was a part of the personal aspect of the narrative line. (Symbolically, humanity {through Prometheus' character} does not wish to self or mass destruct, although the discourse on this notion of self and mass destruction continues all over the world in one conflagration after another.) The sense of individual assertiveness and the sense of positive competition are other personal aspects of the Promethean character.

Within Hesiod, the details given to describe Prometheus and his life are details which ultimately indicated Zeus's own final demise, ironically, as king of the gods and as king of thought. Forethought may, therefore, be seen as the most powerful and important kind of thought of all.

More detail is paid to the construction of Pandora in Hesiod's text—detail and more great glee than one might expect compared to the very few details to the valuable issue of cognition and its potential interactive networks. However, one ought not to underestimate the potential relevant gender issues represented by the exploitation of women (symbolically) within that seeming glee, and the hidden nature of its negative competitiveness, ultimately. In having Pandora created by the great fire-stoker Hephaestus, Zeus ironically had decided against having her forged from fire (not very insightfully) but she is, nonetheless, linked to it. Then Zeus had Hermes breathe great "evils" into her, plainly making them the evils of both Zeus and Hermes, and not of Pandora. She is their repository, their walking, talking computer: a real artificial intelligence. That which is artificial within her is symbolically leveled by the acceptance and love of Epimetheus.

The detail paid to the incest theme of the texts, portrayed most dramatically through Zeus' family line, is another powerful remnant of the Hesiod texts ideologically. Too, as noted earlier, the marriages of brothers and sisters seem to produce erratic behavior among relatives, no matter on what economic level, monarchical on down. Zeus and Hera, brother and sister, man and wife, were the product of Cronos and Rhea, themselves brother and sister, man and wife; Cronos and Rhea were the product of Earth and Heaven, whom presented the variation of mother and son. The reasons for our incest taboos are clearly indicated symbolically and could not be made more obvious except on this literal-physical level, too.

Intrapsychically, returning to the issue of thought and cognition, the most compelling of issues, these three types of thought are part of one's psyche allegorically— one symbolically has Zeus thought, (as a parallel to Freud's super ego or "over I" as Bruno Bettleheim has translated the German) charged with the power of id energy, through linkages with Haephestus and Hermes. Prometheus, as the positive ego (or "I") as a stand-in for all persons or good thinking (symbolically), seems to be struggling for balance in difficult circumstances, especially familial ones. Prometheus is portrayed as willing to make compromises for changed behavior, as one might presume a good ego to be willing to do; too, he does not marry a close relative. Epimetheus, on another level, that middle person (besides being one symbol of the charged libido), is a doubting-Thomas who stands between the desire to change and the desire to stay the same, or that part of the psyche which is willing to find scapegoats, like Pandora, and to be wed to the negative implications of that choice. However, he is, too, just a reminder that change is not easy, a well-known fact.

Extrapsychically, within the narrative, Zeus and Prometheus have been seen, at first, as dialectical opposites, whether to be paralleled symbolically and politically (representing different kinds of thinking) within the Greek city-state. Later, textually, their behavior seems to indicate that they actually seem to be seeking *synthesis* within the undermeanings of the allegory in spite of what seems to be literally happening in the narrative. There may have been denials made by them, had Hesiod chosen to explicate any part of this aspect of the narrative,

but their behavior indicates that they are seeking resolution, not just catharsis.

Aeschylus brings to light the actual *struggle for synthesis* in his *Prometheus Bound* and in the fragments and
bibliographic evidence left of his *Prometheus Unbound*
(Scully 99-110). Aeschylus brings readers and audiences
to this synthesis of elements having both Prometheus and
Zeus as victors. Percy Shelley will later, and hoping to
avoid a synthesis in his *Prometheus Unbound*, have
Prometheus forgive Zeus, but, therefore and thereafter,
not allow Zeus as victor. But Aeschylus' Prometheus is
freed and awarded the flower garland to wear around his
neck; given by Athena (as noted in remains of the
Prometheus Unbound), it is a symbol of the pain of his
"enchainment," but, too, is a symbol of the transformation from the enchainment. This transformation is signed
by the analogous encirclement of both the chain and the
garland; but the garland is a mark of victory over the
pain and guilt which Prometheus may have felt. If there
were feelings of guilt, he moved beyond them. Thus, in
Aeschylus the chaos of the world is seen as capable of
being brought closer to wisdom or balance, a rationality
through the interplay of natural forces. That Zeus felt
sympathy at all (thirteen generations past the child born
to Io) in allowing Heracles (Hercules) to unbind
Prometheus, within the *Prometheus Unbound*, is an indication that he is brought closer to the human level, to
Prometheus, his relative and "becoming" equal—as this
progression indicates.

The question of Aeschylean authorship of the
Promethei cannot be avoided, as textual research indicates its importance and shows, as well, an example of
the nature of research in this area. Oliver Taplin in *The
Stagecraft of Aeschylus* states that he does not believe
Prometheus Bound to be a work of Aeschylus because of
what he calls:

> dramatic techniques which I find inexplicably unlike
> Aeschylus as we know him from other plays . . .
> (Taplin 240)

Lois Spatz in her *Aeschylus* feels that:

the arguments against total Aeschylean authorship are
too strong to be ignored. (144)

She cites Taplin's reasoning, or conjecture, that Aeschylus
completed half of the play (but the whole of the
Prometheus Unbound) in Sicily, for production there, and
then died in 456/5 B.C. Taplin feels that the *Bound* was
then finished by an admirer. Taplin disagrees with C. J.
Herington's acceptance of the *Prometheus Bound*, in spite
of the fact that Herington and Scully present the data
noting the fragmentary references and quotes from the
Prometheus Unbound, the whole of which has been assumed to be lost to us from post-Aeschylean centuries.
Taplin "feels" strongly as he expresses it, that the play
is definitely not of Aeschylus' authorship, although he
notes that other scholars feel just as strongly that it is.

    Spatz thinks it does not matter if Aeschylus did or
did not write the play or the trilogy (some think dilogy).
What matters, she continues, is that Aeschylus was so
admired that someone would use his name, or want to.
It might be fruitful to speculate about why an author
would want to submerge his or her identity to do so,
but Spatz does not so speculate. She does, however, suc-
cumb seemingly, to her own belief that the *Prometheus
Bound* is the work of Aeschylus, but she is unwilling to
be explicit about this. Herington and Scully, on another
track, suggest that structurally the first play of the
Euminides is similar to *Prometheus Bound*. If, they conjecture, the last two plays of the *Euminidies* were elimi-
nated or had been lost, the reader or audience would be
left with the same kind of suspense that one is left with
at the end of the *Prometheus Bound* (that is with no obvious ideological resolution). And Anthony J. Podlecki in
his *The Political Background of Aeschylean Tragedy* states,
simply, that the evidence is strongly for Aeschylean authorship to date.

    Aeschylus makes interesting changes, in terms of
family position, in the *Prometheus Bound* of the Hesiod
Zeus-Prometheus-Epimetheus-Fire paradigm at the same
time that he keeps certain of the elements. In the *Bound*,
summarily, Prometheus becomes, instead of the son of
Iapetus and Clymene ("the neat-ankled maid, daughter

of Ocean"), the son of Themis and Iapetus. Herington and Scully assume that Themis is Earth, and thus make the assumption that Prometheus is a Titan. Hesiod states that Themis is the daughter of Earth and, therefore, herself a Titan. If Prometheus had been a Titan, he would have had a different relationship with Zeus, a closer one. However, Hesiod *does* in the *Theogony* note that Themis and Zeus father some very important children together:

> Horae (Hours), and Eunomia (Order), Dike (Justice), and blooming Eirence (Peace), who mind the works of mortal men, and the Morae (Fates) to whom wise Zeus gave the greatest honor; Clothos, Laachesis and Atropos who give mortal men both good and evil to have. (Evelyn-White 145)

Thus, Zeus and Prometheus are linked subtly here by Aeschylus into another kinship connection. These allegorical and metaphoric children would be both second cousins and, also, half-sisters to Prometheus, using the Aeschylean genealogy against that of Hesiod; therefore, he expands the complexity of the genealogy.

Besides this, there are other textual questions which arise in the Aeschylus *Bound* concerning Themis. Early in the *Bound*, Prometheus calls out to "Earth, mother of us all," making clear the symbolic link to Prometheus' *grandmother* as mother, symbolic mother to all, not only to himself. He later talks of "My mother, Themis, who is also called Earth". Later (1 1334), Prometheus returns to Themis, whom he regards as a Titan: "The Titan Themis, my mother born in archaic time" (Scully 72). And within Hesiod, Prometheus' mother was a Titan, but she was not Themis. Prometheus was, again, correct in identifying the Titans as who they really were, when hoping to avert war, he goes to "the Titans—the sons of Father Sky and Mother Earth—and went for nothing." As well, at line 605, the Aeschylean chorus compare Prometheus to Atlas, his brother, whom they erroneously identify as a Titan. The word Titan means "strainer" and in the chorus/Atlas context, their usage of calling Atlas a Titan could be metaphorical.

However, the internal textual inconsistency concerning the genealogy of Themis is interesting for several reasons, not the least of which would be the attempt of Aeschylus, if this is not a transmission error, to elevate Prometheus to the level of Zeus' uncle, using the assumption of Themis as Earth in Herington and Scully, instead of as his cousin, as in Hesiod. Too, having Prometheus' mother as Earth, aligns him further with the home of mankind/womankind, those for whom he advocated within Hesiod. If this is a conscious ambiguity, it works symbolically for the audience of the *Bound*. Aeschylus incorporates Ocean and his children into the choral group, a backup group for Prometheus. This group would include Clymene, who Hesiod has as Prometheus' mother. It is to the members of the chorus that Prometheus expresses his emotions and ideas, as they do, likewise, to him. It will be seen that other authors within the literary history of this theme change the position of Prometheus in ways which indicate more power for Prometheus. They do, in short, for him what he has done for them as a character within a text—advocate on his behalf as a god, a friend of the human race. His authors become his advocates, and, in so doing, acknowledge healthy, constructive self love, by incorporating what Prometheus represents.

In other ways, Aeschylus broadened the Zeus-Prometheus-Fire paradigm, which it becomes in the *Bound*, because nothing is seen or heard of Epimetheus therein. Firstly, he enlarged upon the narrative structure by taking a small part of Hesiod's work, a complex creation story or rendering of ancient religion, and created a most compelling, dynamic drama. His addition of the chorus marks an historical theatrical stylistic change, and his development of character through dialogue helps the postmodern to see how seriously he takes the intention of this aspect of the text, his reification and heightened deification of Prometheus. His work stands out as a literary/dramatic masterpiece, and marks the construct as a literary historical theme.

As well, within the tragedy, Aeschylus gives Prometheus credit for giving *hope* to mankind/womankind, a great change from Hesiod's giving the hope left in Pandora's jar—a slim hope for womankind one might imagine. In this sense, Pandora is relieved from her bad mother, bad woman role, with Aeschylus' projection for Prometheus. Too, the addition of Io as a character to the drama heightens interest in the future salvation/freedom of Prometheus and strengthens the tension of Zeus' proposed denouement.

Io and the child she bore are the forerunners of Heracles, the liberator of Prometheus, as noted earlier. Prometheus' liberation will relieve society of the need for the antithetical monarchical, plebeian concept. As well, it re-elevates woman as well, symbolically. Io is released through her progeny from the slavery (as a heifer) which had been forced upon her by monarchy, through Rhea (the Greek Hera). Her union with Zeus, too, is an indication of the need for exogamy, and a remove and release from incest which has been obvious in the pantheon.

The enormous groundwork developed by Aeschylus toward an understanding of the need for the democratic sensibility cannot be underestimated. Within his *Bound* Prometheus suffered, but never ceased to struggle with his prescient knowledge of Zeus's destiny. Zeus's replacement, or removal, should have been no greatly "new" news, considering the mytho-psychic precedents seen in the denouements of other king gods within the pantheon, of both his father and grandfather. Aeschylus is quite bold in his explication, which is developed through dialogue, of an underlying ethic of democratic "civil" principle.

From the repository of the bibliographic remnants gathered by Herington and Scully of the *Prometheus Unbound*, we can feel the dialectical tension of Zeus and Prometheus, relatives at war, brought to an ultimate conclusion in which both characters are freed from their fear and indulgence in destruction, dialectical destruction on the figurative level, appeased synthetically through struggle. The flower garland (as a symbol of liberation for Prometheus and the human psyche), worn by him around his neck after it was presented to him by Athena, goddess of wisdom, is a symbolic representation of freedom from guilt for assertive behavior for those for whom he had advocated all along, his beloved humans. The passage wherein Prometheus states in the *Unbound* of Zeus

> He's savage, I know. He keeps
> justice in his fist.
> But with this hammer blow
> He'll soften, He'll calm down
> His blind stubborn rage.
> He'll come to me, as a friend
> I'll love my friend again. (Scully 38-39)

clearly signifies a reality within the drama of an intended resolution. If one accepts the bibliographic evidence of the accompanying plays to the *Prometheus Bound* (Scully 99-110), as this author does, then the final floral tribute is not only a tribute to the Promethean nature, but it is also a tribute to the mind which conceives of love as a guiding principle wherein the labor of love through action, as typified in the word, (the spoken word, the written word, the prophetic word, the caring word, and the word of meaning). This kind of a nature and mind is rewarded by a community of other minds with gratitude and thanks.

Mary Shelley will transform her Prometheus into a human being. This some may see as a denouement for Prometheus. She, however, develops her Prometheus as an experimental doctor, an early forerunner of the geneticist and the test-tube, baby-making obstetrician, symbolically. Her imagination keeps Prometheus alive as a literary character in another context, but one which bears thematic similarities, even if different allegorical and metaphoric interpretations are the end result.

VICTOR FRANKENSTEIN, II, OR SATAN MINUS SATAN: MARY SHELLEY'S PRESCIENT INSIGHTS

Fragment

O Mary dear, that you were here
With your brown eyes bright and clear,
And your sweet voice, like a bird
Singing love to its lone mate
In the ivory bower disconsolate;
Voice the sweetest ever heard!
And your brow more . . .
Than the   sky
Of this azure Italy.
Mary, dear, come to me soon,
I am not well whilst thou art far;
As sunset to the sphered moon,
As twilight to the western star,
Thou, beloved, art to me.
O Mary dear, that you were here;
The castle echo whispers "Here!" (Bennesen 109)

–Percy Shelley
Este, Italy, Sept. 1818

One way for a reader to imitate Percy Shelley's invocation, to echo "here" and to have her near, is to reach for Mary Shelley's first book, *Frankenstein, A Modern Prometheus* published in 1818. Although Mary Shelley did not have strong convictions concerning her talent, she tells of her husband's encouragement in an Appendix to *The Cenci*, the Appendix written after his death:

> He often incited me to attempt the writing of a trag-
> edy: he conceived that I possessed some dramatic
> talent, and he was always most earnest and energetic
> in his exhortations that I should cultivate any talent
> I possessed. (Duerksen 109)

She did succeed in cultivating that talent, although she
herself was not convinced of her own talent. Her first
book *establishes the Prometheus theme in a radically pro-
fane setting*, developing the Promethean allegory very
complexly for postmodern man and woman, and the modern artist of 1818.

In her expansion and transformation of Hesiod's allegory viewed abstractly, her remarks about the artist and
scientist include exhortations and suggestive implications
to the reader of the potential danger associated with creativity, and the act of creation, both at the physical and
abstract levels. A kind of nascent fear, if not preconscious,
symbolic conscious fear of creativity gets established
which carries with it an ambivalent tenor. This seems to
be all the more valid for Shelley, as part of the idea for
her book came from a dream she had at the time when
she was contemplating writing. Artistic and scientific ac-
complishment can be hazardous to the artist and the
scientist, but also to those close to the artist/scientist:
including men, women, and children of all ages if one
looks symbolically at what becomes of those affiliated with
Victor Frankenstein, just because he is Frankenstein the
doctor/scientist/artist/father. The object of art, or creation, too, is in danger of both being misunderstood and
destroyed. The art and artist, however, are both open to
understanding and comprehension to those open to understanding and struggling with comprehension. Mary
Shelley is able to establish her ideas without using the
Classic, poetic form of ancient Greece. Percy will revert
to the Classical style, one of his favorite forms later in
his *Prometheus Unbound* (published two years after his
wife's book), but imitation of the Classical was primary
to Percy.

At its most elemental level, Mary Shelley's *Frankenstein* incorporates Prometheus into the being of a man.
This marks the leap from pantheon, a projected idea from

mind, back into the soul and mind of one member of humanity. This idea, or potential projection, is latent in Hesiod and Aeschylus. Victor Frankenstein metaphorically represents the link from the ancient past, from seeming etherial beginnings, to one of the archetypal modern tragic heroes of fiction. Victor is an inherently flawed character, but flawed for reason or reasons which are implicitly and explicitly expressed. Early in the narrative, part of Victor's tragedy, or his tragic-flaw, is revealed. His flaw is involved with the facts that his parents "worshiped" him and that he had a "temper"—as compared with other children around him, with whom he was growing up, who seemed angelic or good to the highest degree. As such, he, too, may be a reflection of Percy Shelley's early childhood and adolescence, as has been noted by other scholars.

Mary Shelley's book is quite influenced by Christianity, as one would expect it to be, post Classical, as it is; however, the Classics, obviously, do not go unnoticed by her, as the theme of her book would indicate and her private studies (both with and without her husband) of the Classics have indicated. One of the most important aspects of her book concerns the "evil" of intellect, which we assume to be related to the forbidden fruit of the garden, the tree of knowledge and death, and the consequences of the forbidden eating indulgence. The good people in her text are structurally deemed to be those *without temper*, by Victor, himself. Although all of Victor's friends are as intellectual as he is, and one would suppose, post Lapsarian-like, doomed as he is without some final mitigating Christian belief on his part.

Furthermore, Shelley's book seems to answer, or wish to, many questions arising from the influences of both the French and American revolutions (and the questions of her own influenced life, having had both the mother and father whom she did). Some of these hypothetical questions include: "What is freedom?"; "What is slavery?"; "Can there be a perfect scientific revolution?" In some ways, her book also seems to be willing to grapple with the question of "What is it to be human?"

Within her text, she seems to symbolically continue

with the kinds of questions of such figures as Thomas Paine and Edmund Burke. But also seeing the influences of both Hesiod and Aeschylus upon Mrs. Shelley's book is not enough to see. There are other influences which show themselves within the metaphors and analogies which are used structurally in the text. Other authors whose works influence her text are Dante Allighieri (*Inferno*), Charles Brockden Brown (*Wieland; or The Transformation, Ormond*, and *Arthur Merwyn; or, Memoirs of the Year 1793*), Samuel Taylor Coleridge (*The Rhyme of the Ancient Mariner*), John Milton (*Paradise Lost*), Johann Wolfgang von Goethe (*Faust*), Erasmus Darwin (*Zoonomia*), her mother Mary Wolstonecraft (*A Vindication of the Rights of Women*), her father William Godwin (*Caleb Wiliams or Things As They Are*, and *An Enquiry Concerning Social Justice*), and Percy Shelley ("Alastor or the Spirit of Solitude", "The Daemon of the World", "Queen Mab", and *The Revolt of Islam)*.

Sandra Gilbert and Susan Gubar discuss some of Mary's influences which they perceive and explicate in their own text, the fascinating *The Madwoman in the Attic*. They are concerned to an important degree with Mrs. Shelley's own biography. Their clear explication that aspects of her autobiography are present in her text helps readers and critics to enlarge the intertextual and cross-textual implications to the text, even to the personal canvas of her life.

However, the Classical constructs remain, "pagan" or not, within Shelley's book, as strong and as important as the Christian influences are structurally. These, plus the intellectual influences upon her work of other authors, make quite a feast for those who do not view intellect as evil, and for those who realize that art inspires more art (and scientific discovery more scientific discovery), or, often, more insight for those who like to decode texts, for relevancy to the ancient past.

Her story is quite moving on most levels of the narrative. Victor Frankenstein's creation, his child, named within this essay as Victor Frankenstein, II, deserves a name because his text is about his development, to some degree, and because his father does not give him a name.

By naming him, one symbolically names the responsibility of his parentage and his parenting. But Victor, his father, like father Earth of Hesiod's text, finds his own son repulsive to him, and wishes to be finished with him. The child of Victor is reminiscent of those of Hesiod's characters, like the orb-eyed Cyclops and the children of the fifty-heads-and-one-hundred-arms. Unfortunately for Victor, perhaps, II could not be remanded to caves within the earth, although II does live hidden for some time in a cave-like construction. Unfortunately for II, he became monstrous to his creator the moment he first breathed, much as humans seemed to Zeus.

The *idea* of creating life, which reveals Victor's Platonic sensibilities, was more wonderful to him than the actual creation, the completed character. At some level, then, his child was a fantasy until the act of creation was completed. Victor was in absolute joy as he was in the act of creating, that much pragmatic involvement is clear. He loathed the "ugliness" of his child at its life; but was this a projection of some inner sense of ugliness of his own? His loathing was quite as Zeus loathed the wickedness which was perceived by him of humankind. Was that a wickedness inherent in *thought* itself, unreflective thought, allegorically? But II, in contradistinction to Zeus' misbehaving humans (as he perceived them), had at the moment of his creation shown *no* vice. He was an innocent who was rejected just as his ancient ancestors had been, intertextually and cross-textually, the children of Earth.

The ambivalent tenor of the feelings associated with creation, and "no desire" for responsibility for the children, is familiar to readers both from Hesiod and from Aeschylus. Too, the idolatry of Victor by his parents is a familiar motif from both Homer and Virgil. Even though a rather tarnished figure in his own eyes, Victor has that element of the heroic from the ancient past with both the temper, noted earlier, and the motifs, often herein symbolic, associated with the heroic. His parents are like the suppliants who worshipped the god (Zeus) with a temper. Zeus clearly felt ambivalently towards many of his fellow gods and goddesses, although he did elevate some. He did especially feel ambivalence toward anyone whom he felt might take his place, or try to supplant him, like a jealous and insecure father or mother might.

Victor, also, felt (late in the narrative) that if he created a mate for Victor II, then the children, if there were any from that match, might one day rule the world. In one sense, too, Mary Shelley's book is prophetic in that it points to a distant biogenetic future wherein the fears of that biochemically created "other" or biologically created other, represents a seemingly true unknown ethically, morally, and physically to any otherwise ordinarily created individual. However, her book could be dealing on one level with her own projected fear, or wish (or both), that birthing might one day be taken out of the hands/bodies of women. Clearly, her text is rich with potential interpretation in that wise.

Further, we cannot forget that Mary Wolstonecraft Godwin Shelley lived historically close in time to the American and French revolutions. Her mother participated in the French revolution and wrote about her experiences, as well as about the failures of accountability of that revolution. Her father's philosophical reactions are well known. As well, the prophetic mood of the *Theogony*, the *Works and Days*, and the *Prometheus Bound* speak of the denouement of monarchy within the universe. The denouement of monarchy (which was highlighted during her mother's lifetime, and Godwin's), helped to activate Mary's reuse of the theme of Zeus-Prometheus-Epimetheus-Fire, with its many afterthoughts (Epimetheus as they might be), and to encourage its usage, for meaning, in her novel. Victor's son is also Pandora-like, and in spite of what finally happened to Victor and his son, there is hope from II's creation—something left from his invisible jar of evil abuses and psychological ills. Just as the French revolution created what seemed a new democratic monster (to replace the monarchy), a new form of symbolic slavery was born from that upheaval, as well. People longing for freedom are often caught in a kind of time warp; longings for freedom were not quite so easily put into a new place after the revolution—so aspects of serfdom were lingering, and other tyrants stood at the door of power, other than the members of monarchy whom were presumed to be the evil ones at the time of change. The new Democrats were not instantaneously enlightened with their freedom—with the downfall of the monarchy and "absolutely everything else" it seemed. Just so, even before Prometheus could be freed from his mountain enchainment, he endured much suffering, and in the truest sense, one could say his was not either a self-imposed suffering, but one which was clearly imposed upon him by his monarchy. His regeneration from his suffering was equally as relentless as the suffering itself, even though it may have appeared as a spontaneous reaction; it was not.

So, too, did II suffer, a suffering which seemed inspired by his father's rejection of him. He did not kill with "ape-like fury" as Robert Louis Stevenson's *Dr. Jekyl and Mr. Hyde* would, although when Stevenson wrote, Charles Darwin's evolutionary theory was well established. (When Mary and Percy were writing, they were influenced by Darwin's grandfather, Erasmus, who hinted at all that Charles Darwin would discover). But Mary Shelley's II did kill, and killed out of what would appear as fury and revenge for rejection by his father. His malice was born, as well, from the constant rejection for superficial visual responses on the part of his many rejecters. That is, everyone found II to be too much "the other;" but basically that meant that everyone found him too big and too ugly, as *ugly* was defined (as it seems to be in every period by certain fallible aesthetic standards).

The greatest irony and tragedy were that this projected loathing by others of II got through to him. When he saw his own reflection in a reflecting pool, he, too, saw only that which he felt was ugly and horrid. The reactions of individuals within society had served as his first reflective pool. He had already conceived of the "others" as the beautiful ones and he accepted their projection of his difference. He did not realize that really beautiful people, as he had unconsciously fantasized them to be, did not exist, or were yet to be met within this text, or in the world at large. II often felt so saddened when alone, and felt that if only others would talk to

him, or stop to listen to him, they would find him refined and then find him acceptable. His form, however,
seemed to inspire behavior exemplified by ritualized
scapegoating which was obvious in the Greek pantheon
and city/state. There seemed to be no other cultural
norms as to why, or reason why, the rejecters rejected
II; they just could not grasp his beauty through the enormous visual differences in comparison to themselves.
Cultural evolution had not yet arrived to that point historically, for such a cognitive birthing, such a release from
chains.

Too, Victor's child did not have a mother to love him,
and perhaps this was one of Mary Shelley's concerns
about these futuristically-conceived children; they might
not know or feel true mother love, which goes beyond
such outward physical-feature casting, or it can. II just
did not seem human to other humans; he was taller than
most of them (between seven and eight feet). He was made
of the body parts of other humans (supposedly already
dead ones) as akin to our postmodern organ transplants,
but he was endowed with a brain and a fine capacity for
reason. Too, Victor had his child electrically charged to
bring him to life—like Zeus of the lightning and thunder,
he worked his wonders.

Both Shelleys were aware of the work of Erasmus
Darwin, as noted earlier, and they made use of it. It has
been said of this earlier Darwin that

> If Erasmus had a pervasive though unconscious in-
> fluence over Charles, there should be plenty of par-
> allels between *Zoonomia* and the *Origin of Species*.
> There are: almost every topic discussed in *Zoonomia*
> and every example given, reappears in the *Origin*.
> (King-Hele 68)

Erasmus Darwin, for instance, hypothesized:

> that nerve impulses were electrical a fact which was
> not established until after 1850 (68)

and he

> foresaw the importance of electricity at a time when
> it had the status only of a toy. (50-51)

His "foreseeing" links him to Prometheus metaphorically. It is no wonder then that Mary Shelley incorporated Erasmus Darwin's name into the beginning of her book *Frankenstein*. Like Prometheus who borrowed from the pantheon and Zeus, she took a bit of this Erasmus' insightful and symbolic "fire" and toyed with many of his ideas in her book. It was electricity which charged II with life, but just as instantly as he was brought to life, he was, quite sadly, rejected by bad human behavior. Mary Shelley's concerns for beginnings, and reasons for beginnings, also carries weight for love, even on a larger, societal level.

Because of her concerns, she has II create a rationale for his own life, which is quite moving and draws upon the reader's compassion. And quite like Hesiod's Cyclops and those of the fifty-heads-and-one-hundred-arms, he is a victor in his own way in the novel, in spite of the fact that he becomes a murderer within the confines of its pages. He lives beyond the death of his father, for which he was, it seems, partially responsible. He lives ever so lonely and ever so knowledgeably of the world and its ways in the vast cold of the North by the end of the text. Like the early, immature Zeus, he abandoned those whom he perceived to have abandoned him. In fact, II was immolated with self-knowledge and the knowledge of others, which is why he threatens to ignite himself on a pyre in the cold of the North. He is decidedly not like Dante's Satan, nor like Milton's Satan. He is instead, a Satan-minus-Satan, a kind of zero, one among many stimulants to the conscience of the world. He shows us weaknesses, potential weaknesses, and potential social problems—not just his own. He is as well, stylistically, an incredible anti-hero. For someone who began so innocently, after that first burst of life and the first smile from the lips, his was a most tragic fall, quite different from Satan's own; and truly Victor Frankenstein, his father, did not have the magnanimity of either Prometheus or the Judeo-Christian God.

The idea of a reader's having compassion for a fictive murderer is probably one that does not first spring to mind. It seems alien—what about the people he killed, we might rightly ask? In Western society as it has evolved, until arguably postmodern times, the compensation one must pay for killing was punishment, either with the taking of the life of the murderer or of incarceration for a determined length of time, by a judging body. II's punishment, finally, was his total isolation from humanity as he plundered with his dogs and sled further into the cold regions of the Arctic. Belief in the reform of the murderer is slim as the crimes of the murderer are so great. But the particular irony for II was that he, the murderer, rationalized his murders as mimetic murders, by extended metaphor; that is, he felt that society was killing or murdering him. In his primitive way, he was attempting to repay a society which rejects or "murders" on superficial grounds, a society which does not give him opportunity or time to express himself and to finally define himself in humane terms. His virtues are continuously all overlooked. He is damned on the grounds of his appearance, the externals, something he feels innocent of being responsible for, and something for which he is continually trying to compensate. In one sense and at one level, he is a symbol of child abuse and how a child becomes the abuser.

On the figurative level, by killing William (and later Clerval and Elizabeth, after his father Victor kills his future mate), II is himself being the rejecter, and he has assumed the insanity of the rejecting society in the most brutal way to that society. He is rejecting the source of his sorrow and proclaiming his own right to life, his right to be loved and accepted on the basis of his inherent value and intrinsic beauty. In killing the others, most importantly, he is finally rejecting himself, just as the others had rejected him. He had inherited, mimetically, his father's temper and taken it further. He did not learn, or was unable to learn, a symbolic intrapsychic mode in order to be able to cope with the enormously complex and painful issues of his life.

However, as a self-taught being, he still longed for the love of others and in spite of his numerous and appalling rejections. In his dialogue with Walton, near the end of the book, II accepts his final desolation:

Yet I seek not a fellow feeling in my misery. No sympathy may I ever find. When I first sought it, it was
the love of virtue, the feeling of happiness and affection with which my whole being overflowed, that I
wished to be participated . . . Once my fancy was
soothed with dreams of virtue, of fame, and of enjoy-
ment. Once I falsely hoped to meet with beings, who,
pardoning my outward form, would love me for the
excellent qualities which I was capable of unfolding.
I was nourished with high thoughts of love and devo-
tion. But now crime has degraded me beneath the
meanest animal. No guilt, no mischief, no malignity,
no misery, can be found comparable to mine. When I
run over the frightful catalogue of my sins, I cannot
believe that I am the same creature whose thoughts
were once filled with sublime and transcendent visions
of the beauty and the majesty of goodness. But it is
even so; the fallen angel becomes a malignant devil.
Yet even that enemy of God and man had friends and
associates in his desolation; I am alone. (Joseph 221)

II's aloneness is a warning to any future "modern"
Prometheus who would dare attempt to create without
the capacity for compassion and understanding of the
creation.

Just as Dante stands his Satan frozen in hell (seemingly upside down for those descending into the inferno), so Mary Shelley inverts the received perception of
Prometheus into "other" and gives readers provocative
thoughts about that otherness, and any other internal
"otherness" that they might possess themselves. Some of
the motivating undercurrents of her novel, as in Hesiod
and Aeschylus, are related to the quests for knowledge
and discovery either of the marvelous, the alchemistic,
the scientific, the artistic, or the philosophic. Light, as
an indicator of the Zeus-Prometheus-Epimetheus-flame,
is an ever present and constant motif in the book, whether the light is sunlight, light of the seasons, the primary
color of the Arctic, or the lightning bolts from her fictive
sky, to select but a few. Too, each primary character is
attempting to move toward self-knowledge, and the plays
upon light and darkness always involve them.

Captain Walton seeks the experience of the marvelous. Victor Frankenstein wants to experience the marvelous too, and to create life. II, his creation, wanted to be loved, and hoped through his self education that he could receive esteem from others. He had very little self-esteem for himself, partially because of the negative projections of others, but, too, because he accepted those negative projections and did not know how to grow or to evolve beyond them. One could acknowledge that he had not been taught how to cope with these complex issues.

Structurally, the book begins as a series of four letters of correspondence. The remaining portions are a collection of notes (divided into chapters) which Captain Walton takes while listening to Victor Frankenstein tell his tale, for Walton's own sister to read. The mode is confessional, and must be so viewed from the points of view of all of the major characters. Captain Walton writes to his sister, Mrs. Saville (hints of Spain and the international portent of the book) from St. Petersburg and Archangel, both cities of Russia. The reference to St. Petersburg is also a reference to the archangel St. Peter, symbolically. The North, Russia and the Arctic, which Walton seeks, become the oxymoronic heaven/hell of the North, with the combination of the beauty of a paradise and the cold, real aspect of the symbolic frozen pit, wherein Satan flaps his wings of Dante's hell.

In his travels, Robert Walton sought a friend, an intellectual companion. He, himself, was a composite character (Promethean, to a large degree; Medieval like Parzival {Parsifal, Percival}, exploring the boundaries of a wasteland; and, potentially, he was a nature-breaking Faustian). He felt a need to have someone near with whom to confide, other than through the letters to his sister. An ambitious person, he wanted to make new shipping discoveries, find new land, make new connections between lands, and break barriers, all without losing his soul, his spiritual nature. When he and his shipmates found Victor Frankenstein in a dissipated state, worn from chasing his son across the Northland, they took him onto their ship. In Frankenstein, Walton found the friend he had sought for so long:

> I was easily led by the sympathy which he evinced,
> to use the language of my heart; to give utterance to

the burning ardour of my soul; and to say with all the fervour that warmed me, how gladly I would sacrifice my fortune, my existence, my every hope to the furtherance of my enterprise. One man's life or death were but a small price to pay for the acquirement of the knowledge which I sought; for the dominion I would acquire and transmit over the elemental foes of our race . . . at length he spoke 'Unhappy man! Do you share my madness? Have you drank also of the intoxicating draught? Hear me,—let me reveal my tale and you will dash the cup from your lips. (28)

Victor Frankenstein, the Promethean and the Faustian brother, proceeded then to tell his story (which also included his son's story within it), which he described as "marvellous." Captain Walton noted of Frankenstein "his lustrous eyes" as he spoke and "the lineaments of his face are irradiated by the soul within." Captain Walton discovered in Frankenstein "the brother of his heart" who had been in pursuit of II, whom Victor called his daemon. But the "draught" of which Frankenstein spoke is the same kind of symbol, or seeming magical device, as the flame of Zeus-Prometheus-Epimetheus, the apple of Adam and Eve, the love potient of Tristan, the grail of Parsifal, and the "Book of Mystery/ From Nostradamus' very hand" belonging to Doctor Faustus. That "draught," their fantasy potient, their longing, has transformed their lives; they now share the same kind of "madness" or what is perceived of as madness—their desire for more knowledge. One also notes the closeness of the spellings of draught and "drought," for their pursuits, to some degree were barren of a final healthy nourishment which refreshes.

Walton, himself, wanted to be encapsulated in light. He was fascinated by the pole, a kind of heaven where the "sun is for ever visible". He sought a country of "eternal light". Walton wanted to find land never set foot upon by man. His fantasies persuade him that the pole is not "the seat of frost and desolation" supposed. He is intrigued with "the dangerous mysteries of ocean" but "besides this" he has "a love for the marvelous, a belief in the marvelous." He had devoted his nights to the study of mathematics, the theory of medicine, and those branches of physical science from which a naval adventurer might derive the greatest practical advantage. (17)

The captain, like Victor, had a "steady purpose—a point on which the soul might fix its intellectual eye." He even compared himself in his efforts to a poet. He had tried to be a poet for a full year previous to his journey. The reader wonders whether to admire these men or to consider them delusional to a large degree.

Victor's own narrative, similarly, revealed that he had turned to the study of mathematics and the sciences, not from poetry, but from metaphysics; but it did him no good as "destiny" had deemed him to destruction—that is, back to metaphysics. Here the reader notes the structural similarity between the destiny of which he speaks and the Fates (or the fatalism) of ancient Greek mythology, with Aeschylus' "necessity", with the sense of doom of the Anglo-Saxon period, and with the "predestination" concept of John Calvin to grasp its full import.

Too, on the grandest level of Victor's narcissism, he stated:

> It was the secrets of heaven and earth that I desired to learn: and whether it was the outward substance of things or the inner spirit of nature and the mysterious soul of man that occupied me, still my enquiries were directed to the metaphysical, or, in its highest sense, the physical secrets of the world. (37)

Victor associated "good" with mathematics and "evil" with metaphysics. The seeming inevitability of destiny's "immutable laws" had him firmly in "her" grip at the age of fifteen. (Perhaps here, Mary Shelley was actually alluding to her husband's own youth, and absorption with the sciences and metaphysics). But for Victor, at this time he witnessed a most violent and terrible thunderstorm:

> As I stood at the door, on a sudden, I beheld a stream of fire issue from an old and beautiful oak, which stood about twenty yards from our house: and as soon as the dazzling light vanished, the oak had disap-

> peared, and nothing remained but a blasted stump .
> . . I never beheld anything so utterly destroyed . . .
> a man of great research was with us, and excited by
> this catastrophe, he entered on the explanation of a
> theory which he had formed on the subject of elec-
> tricity and galvanism, which was at once new and
> astonishing to me. (41)

The Zeus-Prometheus-Epimetheus-Fire impulse within
Shelley's text was then replaced within the text by the
"spirit of good" which meant a temporary turn by Victor
away from metaphysics to mathematics. Perhaps mathematics seemed more grounded, but Shelley's text bears
the allegorical aegis of Zeus, thunder bolt and lightning
bolt, which becomes linked to science, the electrical and
the galvanic, and, thus, oxymoronically and ironically
associated with both life and death. There is something
mathematical, too, in the consistency and preciseness
within Shelley's use of the ancient paradigm.

Clerval, Victor's dearest friend, too, was associated
with the fire (and its light) of the symbolic Zeus-
Prometheus-Epimetheus-Fire paradigm. He was a com-
poser of songs, a writer of romances (mimetically copying
the Medieval style) and an actor who loved theater. Victor semiotically

> read in his kindling eye and his animated glance a
> restrained but firm resolve, not to be chained to the
> miserable details of commerce. (44)

Thus would this Promethean youth be unbound, and, too,
avoid the burden of guilt from the exploitations of his
father (for Clerval was "the son of a merchant of Geneva")
and too much similitude with the father. Victor had found
a retinue member like himself—someone who strove to
break with the past presciently with a bit of foreknowledge, no matter how unenlightened.

At Ingolstodt, the school where Victor went to continue his education, he created II while just a student.
Much light imagery is used by the authoress after Victor
decides to "pioneer a new way" while "treading in the
steps already marked":

> I paused, examining and analyzing all the minutae of causation, as exemplified in the change from life to death, and death to life, until from the midst of this darkness a sudden light broke upon me—a light so brilliant and wondrous, yet so simple, (Joseph 52-57)
>
> . . .
>
> I became myself capable of bestowing animation on lifeless matter, (52)
>
> . . .
>
> I was like the Arabian who had been buried with the dead, and found a passage to life, aided only by one glimmering, and ineffectual light. (53)
>
> . . .
>
> Life and death appeared to me ideal bounds which I should first break through, and pour a torrent of light into our dark world. A new species would bless me as its creator and source, (54)
>
> . . .
>
> I collected the instruments of life around me, that I might infuse a spark of being into the lifeless thing that lay at my feet, (54)

and

> my candle was nearly burnt out, when by the glimmer of the half-extinguished light, I saw the dull yellow eye of the creature open. (55)

At this moment for Victor

> the beauty of the dream vanished, and breathless horror and disgust filled my heart. (57)

Victor's realization that his pragmatic employment had led to life terrified him because presumably, at one level, his guilt at playing God took over. As well, the difference between fantasy and reality took hold. This Christianized Prometheus of the nineteenth-century was the kind of man whom the ancient Greek Prometheus had rallied for against the desires of Zeus. This very human has become prey in Mary Shelley's work to the frailties of the human form: to delusions of grandeur, desires for fame and discovery, doubt, and morbid curiosity, to name but a few. This "breathless horror and disgust" are a far cry from the same Victor as he perceived of himself as he labored over his creation as "an artist occupied by his favorite employment". Mary Shelley deftly and boldly links the arts, humanities, and the sciences within the emotions and employments of characters.

But Victor's disgust of II was, too, a projection of his inner self-loathing, due to a lack of personal insight, love, and knowledge. Or, to project at another level, was the world ready for artificially created life? II was born unnaturally, just as Athena, Hephaestus, and Eve had been, from one parent. II's innocence is what stands out about him; for like a baby, he fixed his eyes upon Victor:

> His jaws opened and he uttered some inarticulate
> sounds, while a grin wrinkled his cheeks. (58)

Knowing the torture of what happened to II from that time onward, the reader feels that Mary Shelley's novel becomes a symbolic indictment against modern societies and individuals within these societies who would think progressively, but who could not accept the responsibility for the outcomes, or the creations, of their revolutionary-like zeal, whether they were political or scientific in nature.

Everyone in Shelley's book runs from II but Walton. And Walton stands listening to II as he speaks over the corpse of Frankenstein, his father. (He had killed Victor's brother, his uncle, for the sole reason that his last name was Frankenstein.) The reader is moved once again, and saddened at II's masochistic, but all too easily understood, fantasy of death:

> "But soon," he cried, with sad and solemn enthusiasm, "I shall die, and what I now feel be no longer felt. Soon these burning miseries will be extinct. I shall ascend my funeral pile triumphantly, and exult in the agony of the torturing flames. The light of that conflagration will fade away; my ashes will be swept

into the sea by the winds. My spirit will sleep in
peace, or if it thinks, it will not surely think thus.
Farewell." (223)

At that moment, II left Walton and disappeared into darkness. Before he left, he made it clear that he never for-
gave Victor for his rejection. But does the reader forgive
II for the senseless murder of other innocents? II felt that
the world would have been better served had Victor put
his animosities to constructive ends, to helping him, II,
to survive. But does the reader not feel the same for II?
But how could he have put himself to constructive ends
when everyone rejected him because they were afraid of
the way that he looked? Shelley could have had him com-
mit suicide, presumably. However, II's understanding of
regeneration, and faith in the regenerative spirit, ironically seems stronger than that of Victor's, although clearly
not strong enough to help root him constructively in the
world. This understanding, angry and weak as it was,
was perhaps II's only victory; he had fought back but in
a dangerous and non-absolvable way.

The reader as witness to II's knowledge of his
aloneness and masochistic death fantasies can identify
with both, and almost simultaneously, through dramatic
irony, mull over one's own potential (and often probable)
aloneness and occasional, if unwitting, masochistic fantasies which may be attendant upon one's own difficulties in a profoundly complex and ethically confused
society. Mary Shelley does not offer solutions, but leaves
us with some very interesting ideas to ponder. In the
same or similar circumstances, how would/could any of
us behave?

II never had the opportunity to tell his "observers"
that they were "hurting his feelings" because the first
thing that he became aware of, in the midst of perform-
ing some kindly deed, was that they were already run-
ning away from him. Was Victor guilty for the death of
his little brother William, by having created II in the first
place, or through his rejection of II? Both Elizabeth and
Justine felt guilty, as well as did Victor, but not all of
the characters understood the other possible things to
feel guilty for but Victor. The ultimate guilt for the lit-

eral murders was II's, as was evidenced by the profundity of his remorse. He "framed" Justine for the death of William Frankenstein, just as Mr. Falkland had allowed others to die for his crime (the murder of Mr. Tyrell) in *Caleb Williams*. Mr. Falkland, one presumes, should have known better, but others may bear some responsibility for II's profound alienation—his creator, for one, who was his father; the others who interacted with II, or whom had that possibility; society in both its artistic, humanistic, and scientific ignorance; and II, himself, as he did acknowledge. Percy Shelley succinctly stated a potential help to this kind of alienation problem in a description which defines what postmodern psychologists might call identification, or at least one form of it, and empathy:

> The great secret of morals is love; or a going out of our nature, and an identification of ourselves with the beautiful which exists in thought, action, or person, not our own. A man, to be greatly good, must imagine intensely and comprehensively; he must put himself in the place of another and of many others; the pains and pleasures of his species must become his own. (Winstanley 18-19)

The inability to identify II's speciation (Victor thought that he created another species) was ultimately part of everyone's problem. II seemed to think that he was human; but he could not ultimately love himself or others. Most are taught that they must love others as they love themselves; but II was not ever in an environment wherein he could learn forms of healthy self love, or to get the appropriate supports for a good sense of self-esteem. If he had, he would have potentially been able to redirect some forms of his anger. Too, he seemed to have inherited, though we are not sure how, Victor's tendency toward a bad temper, but carried to extreme ends. Infantile rage in the body of a seven- to eight-foot human would be dangerous under any circumstances. It was clear that II wished to kill his father through the murder of William Frankenstein, a displacement figure.

Victor later destroyed II's intended mate—although she was not alive in the truest sense when he did this.

At one juncture, he aborted his efforts after only having partially created her. And, yet, interestingly, he felt no remorse. II's remorse was suprahuman in contrast. Another question arises; that is, what was the greatest crime? Was it Victor's psychological and biological rejection of II, or II's literal unlawful taking of the life of William, and later of the others? Or is it "fair" to make such a comparison? Is it important that these two were both men? Is Shelley making statements symbolically about what might happen with birth in the hands of men alone?

Mary Shelley's understanding that social justice needed honing could not have been more symbolically or tragically expressed than in her first novel. Too, she was reflecting some of her husband's own rejection by his family and by his society, structurally, through its undermeanings, in her novel. The prophetic aspect in the novel of artificially created life, which has led us into the more modern discussions in human genetics, is still debated today, with some positivism, as genetic research continues. Through her novel, she attained the "writing of a tragedy" as her husband had encouraged her. That she may not have conceived of her own talent may finally be irrelevant as she listened to the encouragement, and took pen to hand. The legacy and lessons of her book live on and touch our all too postmodern hearts, even though we struggle with other potential catastrophes—the potential for nuclear holocaust being one (even as the world dismantles nuclear devices), the ultimate potential symbolic and/or literal "evil" extension of the negative flame paradigm of the Zeus-Prometheus-Epimetheus-Fire construct.

Cognitive functioning has evolved, but will it evolve to a level of understanding which is needed to create a constructive society, in all nations? Far from the publication date of her novel and far from her modern Prometheus (Victor Frankenstein, and his ill-fated son), readers ponder the implications inherent in her work. She introduced us to the complexity of character through the inversion of a theme which usually carried an opposite message of projection—Prometheus the bold, good, and beautiful humanist. Therein, perhaps, lies but one aspect of its profound brilliance.

V

THE UNBOUND PROMETHEAN,
PERCY BYSSHE SHELLEY:
THE FIRE FOR WHICH ALL THIRST

Percy Shelley had a passion for reforming. He wished to produce work of the ultimate sort and described his desire thus:

> Should I live to accomplish what I purpose, that is, produce a systematical history of what appear to me to be the genuine elements of human society, let not the advocates of injustice and superstition flatter themselves that I should take Aeschylus rather than Plato as my model. (Zillman 43)

Shelley expected to be under criticism by the "advocates of injustice and superstition" and he expected a great deal of work from himself with his interest in creating a systematical history of the genuine elements of society. And, yet, he does, in his very own way, take Aeschylus' style and the Promethean theme as his models, albeit in a rather Platonic way, in his *Prometheus Unbound*. His mimetic attempts are to have drastically different ends, he felt, than those he presumed Aeschylus' *Unbound* would have had, had it survived in full. Ironically, perhaps, (in tone at least) his Prometheus of his *Unbound* does resemble that Prometheus discovered in the bibliographic remains of Aeschylus' *Unbound*, if ever so slightly, and ever so much more dramatically. But Shelley

> was averse from a catastrophe so feeble of reconciling the Champion with the Oppressor of mankind. (35)

Yet, in Aeschylus' *Unbound* the "Champion" is not reconciled, per se, with the "Oppressor" but rather the "Oppressor" is reconciled with the "Champion," in so many ways and to use Shelley's name projections and appellations.

Shelley's description of Prometheus is one which probably describes himself, Shelley, most suitably in the realm of his personal ideals:

> Prometheus is, as it were, the type of the highest perfection of moral and intellectual nature, impelled by the purest and truest motives to the best and noblest ends. (37)

Many have questioned the morality of Shelley, but his intellectual nature and primary motivations have also been questioned and judged quite harshly, if not as harshly. Yet, Shelley's intellectual integrity, and moral sensibilities, hold their greatest ground in his work for the reader to evaluate for himself or herself. As a poet he was a creator but, too, a creation of his age (Zillman 41). In his provocative discourse on poetics, *A Defence of Poetry*, he describes what a poet is, the responsibility of the poet, the effects of language down to an explication of taste. He states, presuming his own artistic beginning, some thought-provoking summations, some of which will be highlighted later in this chapter:

> In the youth of the world, men dance and sing and imitate natural objects, observing in these actions, as in all others, a certain rhythm or order, in the motions of the dance, in the melody of the song, in the combinations of language, in the series of their imitations of natural objects. For there is a certain order or rhythm belonging to each of these classes of mimetic representation, from which the hearer and the spectator receive an intenser and purer pleasure than from any other: the sense of an approximation to this order has been called taste by modern writers. Every man in the infancy of art, observes an order which approximates more or less closely to that from which this highest delight results: but the diversity is not sufficiently marked, as that its gradations should be

sensible, except in those instances where the predomi-
nance of this faculty of the approximation to the beautiful (for so we may be permitted to name the relation
between this highest pleasure and its cause) is very
great. Those in whom it exists in excess are poets, in
the most universal sense of the word; and the pleasure resulting from the manner in which they express
the influence of society or nature upon their own
minds, communicates itself to others, and gathers a
sort of reduplication from that community. Their language is vitally metaphorical; that is, it marks the
before unapprehended relations of things and perpetu-
ates their apprehension, through time, signs for portions or classes of thoughts instead of pictures of
integral thoughts; and then if no new poets should
arise to create afresh the associations which have
been thus disorganized, language will be dead to all
nobler purposes of human intercourse. These simili-
tudes or relations are finely said by Lord Bacon to
be "the same footsteps of nature impressed upon the
various subjects of the world"—and considers the faculty which perceives them as the storehouse of axi-
oms common to all knowledge. In the infancy of
society every author is necessarily a poet, because
language itself is poetry; and to be a poet is to apprehend the true and the beautiful, in a word, the
good which exists in relation, subsisting, first between
existence and perception and expression. (Winstanley
6-7)

One is variously fascinated by Percy Shelley the creator
and Percy Shelley the social creation. His own exile from
England was partially the experience of multiple rejections by his parents, Oxford University, and his detrac-
tors in the literary marketplace for both his ideas as he
stated them and for his actions with his words. He
seemed to be rejecting the traditions of his family and of
his own age, or so it seemed to others. He seemed at
times to be inventing or creating the world anew in ways
that perhaps only a postmodern audience might be able
to comprehend on a larger scale. While the intention of
this chapter is to highlight the creator, his ideas as a
social creation will sometimes intervene for attention. In
his thirty short years, Shelley created a wished-for soci-

ety in his mind and in his works, one wherein the struggle for love and goodness were as imperative as he perceived them to be. For Shelley, in his *Prometheus Unbound*, unbinds ideas, feelings, and characters which readers would do well to more closely apprehend. His poetry and ideas suggest an unusual awareness of, understanding of, and expression of a simultaneity of action and multiple ideas within experience(s). It will be fruitful to trace a few of these ideas which reoccur in several of his poems, which often are political in nature, to approach understanding of aspects of his narrative iconographies, which have implications for readers to devolve for meaning.

His *Prometheus Unbound*, for instance, is like Hesiod's rendering in the sense that Prometheus and Jupiter (Zeus) are at odds; but Shelley takes Prometheus' side in as antithetical (contrary to his intent or thesis) a way as can be imagined, antithetically to Hesiod's side-taking of Zeus. Shelley's Prometheus, unlike that of Aeschylus', perhaps for obvious reasons, is Christ-like, and far from the Satan whom Shelley feels that he slightly resembles:

> The only imaginary being resembling in any degree Prometheus, is Satan; and Prometheus is in my judgment, a more poetical acter (sic) than Satan, because, in addition to courage, and majesty, and firm and patient opposition to omnipotent force, he is susceptible of being described as exempt from the taints of ambition, envy, revenge, and a desire for personal aggrandisement, which, in the Paradise Lost interfere with the interest. (Zillman 35-36)

It is Shelley's Jupiter (the Roman name for Zeus) who appears as the most Satanic, depicted as he is as a slave holder, revengeful, and as a despot who causes pain. As well, he is not omnipotent, by implications from the climax and denouement of the *Unbound*. Shelley's *Unbound* has twelve more characters (counting the Spirits of the Hours, Echoes, Fauns, Furies, and Spirits as one each, and the Oceanides as three, not including the various Voices and Phantasms) to Aeschylus' eight (counting the chorus as one), and three additional acts, thus encouraging complexity and diversity of thought. His Oceanides are akin to Aeschylus' Chorus, which is composed of daughters of Ocean, and to Hesiod's Clymene (a daughter of Ocean) who is Prometheus' mother in the *Theogony*. Ironically, perhaps, Shelley's Prometheus is, at first, depicted as isolated and strangely alone in his understanding in the universe, much like Mary Shelley's II. Unlike Mary Shelley's II, Percy's Prometheus is relieved of revenge. He is "eyeless in hate" or blind to it. Further unlike II, he shall be relieved of his aloneness by union with another (Asia).

Unlike Aeschylus' Prometheus who was chained to a mountain, Shelley's Prometheus is "nailed to this wall" much as the Nazarene, Christ, would later be nailed to a tree or crucifix (see the Linda Lewis text for the iconography on this issue in reference to both Milton and Blake, especially). Shelley's Prometheus, though not equals in wit to Jupiter within his text, is equal to Jupiter in that they both "see" everything in the universe, all with sleepless eyes, like those of a wide-eyed Argus. Symbolically, they are like the conscious literal mind and the symbolic-conscious mind of, for one example, the dream state, alert to understanding in a special way. Each has seeming priority of seeing, but it is how they interpret and respond to what they see which makes all the difference.

As miserable as Prometheus is in his projected plight and sentence by Jupiter to 3,000 years of being nailed to a wall, he feels it is a far better fate than Jupiter's, which is to reign as a tyrant. Prometheus pities Jupiter, as his own "misery" made him wise to his own rage and helps him to overcome it. It is Prometheus' "agony," which frees him from Jupiter as well as his knowledge of the "time" of the demise of Jupiter. Everyone else but Prometheus is afraid of Jupiter. It is Prometheus' "agony," too, which is Christ-like; he is the self-giving so that others might survive. Jupiter is like Judas, the Pharisees, the Saducees, Pilate, Barabbas. He is in direct touch with hell, as portrayed by Shelley.

Prometheus has one real, initial problem in the *Unbound*. He cannot remember the original curse which he called against Jupiter; he suffers from temporary amnesia. He can only remember walking at one point on earth with his beloved Asia "drinking life from her loved eyes" and his long suffering because of his concerns for humans. He calls upon his mother Earth, another similarity to Aeschylus, to tell him the curse which he cannot remember. She tells him a method to retrieve the information. The method she recommends takes us directly into a stylistic device used by Shelley in his poetics, one of a complex duality system which is somewhat allegorical and which employs mind, body, and the "phantasm" of this world, other world, and a sense of being out of this world.

Several critics have worked diligently to explain Shelley philosophically. Carl Grabo in his interpretation of the *Prometheus Unbound* felt:

> in framing his philosophic system he must needs reconcile science with metaphysics and his faith in social betterment. The task of *Prometheus Unbound* is to fuse these three diverse elements, Revolutionary social philosophy, Platonism or neoPlatonism, and scientific speculation, into a unified whole. He must reconcile materialism and idealism, physics and metaphysics, science and religion.
> . . .
> And to all this must be added as a strain of his thought or as a solvent wherein the other elements of his philosophy were blent, his acceptance of the ethics of Christ,
> . . .
> the ethics of Christ became his and are embodied in his conception of Prometheus . . . (Grabo 10)

An element John Wright adds in his *Shelley's Myth of Metaphor* is that:

> It is everywhere apparent that Shelley's vision of experience has cultural, personal and theoretical dimensions which constitute one of the most nascent and open visions ever to inspire great poetry, and we need to read his words and understand his thought without sacrificing the *indeterminacy* which animated it

and, as he thought, haunted him like Actaeon's
hounds. (Wright 9)

It is in part because of what Wright calls Shelley's indeterminacy that he also defines Shelley as a phen-
omenologist. His subjective reactions became part of his
projections, disguised as they were. While Shelley's philosophy, or combination of philosophies, cannot be underestimated, neither can investigations of his narrative
line (both literal and figurative levels) of his *Prometheus
Unbound*, and other poems which use iconography, iconographical forms, similar structural ideational patterns,
and motifs as the *Unbound* does.

In Act I, on the narrative line, the "phantasm" of
Jupiter (Zeus) as part of Shelley's duality system, is called
out to by Prometheus. Earth has explained to Prometheus
that for every life there is an invisible "shadow" which is
"underneath the grave." When one dies, one is united with
one's shadow. This grave is composed of:

Dreams and the light imaginings of men,
And all that faith creates, or love desires—
Terrible, strange, sublime and beauteous shapes
(Zillman 62)

Prometheus' "ghost" will remember the curse—but Prometheus chose to call the ghost of Jupiter to recall the curse
for him. All that Jupiter's ghost does is to repeat the
curse which entails for Jupiter:

. . .
let a sufferer's curse
Clasp thee, his torturer, like remorse,
Till thine infinity shall be
A robe of envenomed agony
. . .
let the hour
Come, when thou must appear to be
That which thou art internally;
And after many a false and fruitless crime
Scorn track thy lagging fall through boundless space
and time. (67)

In this curse, we recognize Jupiter's Satanic influences, probably from Shelley's readings and parallel usage of Milton's *Paradise Lost*. But after hearing his own curse on Jupiter, Prometheus felt repentant. It was his blind "grief" of the problems of humankind, without his help and fire, which made him so curse as he realized of himself:

> I wish no living thing to suffer pain. (69)

But in his curse, Prometheus also tells the reader that Jupiter has power over all things but

> thyself . . .
> And mine own will. (67)

Prometheus would have Jupiter kiss the blood from his bleeding feet at one level, but, at another, he cannot as he (Prometheus) would disdain "such a prostrate slave."

Thus, ipso facto, the Zoroastrian war of good and evil in the universe is over. Good prevails: but evil presents an amazing tail wind. Art Young feels in his *Shelley and Nonviolence* that:

> As long as Prometheus accepts the efficacy of revenge
> and violence as legitimate modes of human behavior,
> he remains chained to the rock—a rock that repre-
> sents his own limitations . . . (Young 97)

But, the reader feels that it is Prometheus' rage and willingness to suffer, even though seemingly masochistically, which cause him to forget his reason, or rationality, and his own provocation of Jupiter. His grief is this intense. Too, he feels that Jupiter will be overcome with guilt or remorse at his (Prometheus') suffering:

> . . . beholding good
> Both infinite as is the universe, . . . (Zillman 67)

His "Both infinite" again includes Shelley's dualism of good. Good encompasses the duo of Prometheus and his love Asia. Good implies more than one, or the union of two to make one. Community efforts are also imperative to these unions of two. Ione and Panthea stay near Prometheus for Asia's sake:

> Near whom, for our sweet sister's sake
> Ever thus we watch and wake. (63)

The union of male and female is tantamount of the ultimate in much of Shelley's work. Sometimes, as in "Alastor," it is the image of the woman which keeps the male in bliss where no woman exists in physicality. Shelley thus transforms the role of the female in equality to that of the male and brings the lone male image in the Anglo-Saxon poem "Exile" or the "Wanderer" into a new vision. In the *Revolt of Islam*, it is Laon and Cythna whom are equals in physical prowess (in battle as elsewhere), intellectual wisdom, suffering, loyalty to their love, and spiritual union. They reappear after their martyrdom, to tell their story—not as invisible beings, but symbolically as told of the risen Christ, as visible physical presence. Separation is a motif, and endurance of loyalty to the duality is another.

While many of these aspects of the romance are present in the Greek and Medieval romances, in Shelley's work, the equality for and of the female stands out. The idea of duality even suffices for Shelley, with an ultimate union or reunion seen as the goal. In "Prince Athanese" another variation is witnessed as the Prince had:

> . . . wedded Wisdom, and her dower
> Is love and justice (Young 159)

as a personified and allegorized female, reminding one of Boethius' Lady Philosophy. Further, however, Shelley's sense and understanding of duality as strength in the universe appears, also, strikingly within stanzas taken from the *Revolt of Islam* (with the "Dedication" written for Mary Shelley):

> Dedication
> XI
> And what art thou? I know but dare not speak:
> Time may interpret to his silent years.

Yet in the paleness of thy thoughtful cheek,
   And in the light thine ample forehead wears,
   And in thy sweetest smiles, and in thy tears,
And in thy gentle speech, a prophecy
   Is whispered, to subdue my fondest fears:
And through thine eyes, even in thy soul I see
A lamp of vestal fire burning internally. (Hutchison 39)

Canto IV
XXXI
And what was I? She slumbered with the dead.
   Glory and joy and peace, had come and gone.
Doth the cloud perish, when the beams are fled
   Which steeped its skirts in gold? or dark and lone,
Doth it not through the paths of night unknown,
   On outspread wings of its own wind upborne
   Pour rain upon the earth? The stars are shown,
When the cold moon sharpens her silver horn
Under the sea, and make the wide night not forlorn. (78-79)

Dedication
XIV
Truth's deathless voice pauses among mankind!
   If there must be no response to my cry—
If men must rise and stamp with fury blind
   On his pure name who loves them,—thou and I,
   Sweet friend! can look from our tranquility
Like lamps into the world's tempestuous night,—
   Two tranquil stars, while clouds are passing by
Which wrap them from the foundering seaman's sight,
That burn from year to year with unextinguished light.
(40)

The kind of love that Shelley is reflecting upon in these three stanzas, written in 1817 and printed in 1818, is preparatory for the love of Prometheus and Asia in his *Unbound*, written during 1818 and 1819 and published in 1820. In stanza XI of the dedication to Mary Shelley, Percy feels solace because of the wisdom he sees in all of her being. In Canto IV, stanza XXXI, Laon finds a body which he feels might be that of the missing Cythna (although it is not) and reflects upon an identity, devoid of her presence at that time in his life. Structurally, it appears to be a companion piece to the XI segment of the

Dedication. It is also a stanza which reflects great strength in the face of loss, but structurally and thematically also seems bound to stand with stanza XIV of the dedication to Percy's own wife as a continuation of the questioning of each identity. The questioning of personal identity is strong. The link with stanza XIV of the Dedication brings together the two elements of the identification of male and female to unite in the duo noted above (and its seeming divine and mystical oneness):

> On his pure name who loves them,—thou and I,
> Sweet friend! can look from our tranquility
> Like lamps into the world's tempestuous night, . . .
> (40)

Like Prometheus and Asia, united as one, they love humankind. However, Shelley's duo is not always male and female. Sometimes the construct is male-male, female-female, structural aspects of the neuter, or a variation of all. Social, intellectual discourse for communication is paramount in Shelley's work, whether it is for agreement or disagreement, and feelings combined with intelligence are the undercurrent of all.

The conversation between Prometheus and Mercury in Act I is parallel to the conversation of Prometheus and Hermes in the last scenes of Aeschylus' *Bound* in which Hermes chides Prometheus, and assents to his remorseful and thankless task of harassing Prometheus further. But Shelley's Mercury asks Prometheus a similar question as that of Aeschylus' Hermes, but a question with a twist. He asks the length of Jupiter's reign, since Prometheus has that special knowledge. Mercury also tells Prometheus that he pities him, to this response:

> Pity the self-despising slaves of Heaven,
> not me, within whose mind sits peace serene. (Zillman
> 77)

In other words, Shelley has Prometheus telling Mercury to pity himself, and others, as Prometheus has no need of pity even though he is the one who is literally pinioned, because spiritually he is free. The "slaves of Heaven" are the pawns of Zeus.

Act II is the unfolding of the beauty, divinity, and loyalty of Asia. It is a natural narrative move that Prometheus shall love Asia, a personified geographical region; the pantheon is affiliated with Greece and Rome, and Prometheus as part of the god heraldry, must love something earth-like, the personified and geographical Asia, which is certainly one cradle for Greece, from which the West derives so much of its poetic and metaphorical origins as they were subsumed syncretically by Rome. But Asia's beauty is so great that even nature responds to it. She meets, with her sister Panthea, Demogorgon (whose name represents the mythic figure who presides over the netherworld) in the "depth of the deep", a cave within the earth. Demogorgon understands the secrets of the universe, and his being is described by Asia as

> . . . a mighty darkness
> Filling the seat of power, and rays of gloom
> Dart round, as light from the meridian sun,
> Ungazed upon and shapeless: neither limb
> Nor form, nor outline; yet we feel it is
> A living spirit . . . (135)

Demogorgon, who is described as something physicists might recognize as akin to an attempt to anthropomorphize a black hole, metaphorically, reveals himself to be "Eternity" in Act III when he ascends to Jupiter and states:

> . . . Demand no direer name.
> Descend, and follow me down the abyss.
> I am thy child, as thou wert Saturn's child,
> Mightier than thee; and we must dwell together
> Henceforth in darkness. Lift they lightnings not.
> The tyranny of Heaven none may retain,
> Or reassume or hold, succeeding thee:
> Yet if thou wilt—as 'tis the destiny
> Of trodden worms to writhe till they are dead—
> Put forth thy might. (159)

Thus, Percy Shelley eliminates the chief leader of the pantheon monarchy and replaces him (Zeus' tyrannical thought, like that of Freud's potentially dangerous superego) with an invisible presence which can be felt—an absent presence, Demogorgon, a potential symbolic consciousness for the mind, one residence of thought. Too, Jupiter is to be beneath the earth in a Haedes' like place. And instead of separating from the father, as Zeus had done from Saturn (or Cronos), Demogorgon and Jupiter shall dwell together, quite unlike Shelley and his own father.

Also, within Act III, Hercules appears from "nowhere," as his genealogical moment had come, and unbound Prometheus, who then joined with Asia. Only love in the universe is finally immutable for Shelley. Demogorgon speaks to Prometheus in Act IV:

> These are the spells by which to reassume
> An empire o'er the disentangled Doom.
> To suffer woes which Hope thinks infinite;
> To forgive wrongs darker than death or night;
> To defy power which seems omnipotent;
> To love, and bear; to hope, till Hope creates
> From its own wreck the thing it contemplates;
> Neither to change, nor falter, nor repent:
> This like thy glory, Titan, is to be
> Good, great and joyous, beautiful and free:
> This alone Life, Joy, Empire, and Victory. (233)

No longer are sons and fathers to be separated by their anxieties of influence, either way—father to son, or son to father. Thus, too, life/joy/empire/ and victory for the human race and for Shelley's neoPlatonic self become not monarchy, but the expression of love and the absence of aloneness. At least two are for the world in union with each other and friends: Asia and Prometheus-equals in love and life. There is to be no more war, but a finely wished for peaceable kingdom, and primarily, seemingly democratic at that.

In the months and days before Shelley was to die in his Italian exile at the age of thirty, he saw several "phantasms" and had several prophetic dreams. He saw a phantasm of Allegra, his niece, the daughter of Lord Byron and his sister-in-law, Claire Clairemont. He saw the phantasm of Allegra, two weeks after her death at the age of five, as he walked on an Italian beach with Edward Williams (with whom he would drown just two months later). Allegra was naked, and seemed to rise among the "breakers of the sea". She clapped her hands "as in joy, smiling at him". Shelley adored Allegra; and he had written of her in 1818 in "Julian and Maddalo" (wherein she lived into late, mature years):

> A lovelier toy sweet Nature never made,
> A serious, subtle, wild yet gentle being,
> Graceful without design and unforeseeing,
> With eyes—oh speak not of her eyes!—which seem
> Twin mirrors of Iralian Heaven, yet gleam
> With such deep meaning as we never see
> But in the human countenance: with me
> She was a special favourite: I had nursed
> Her fine and feeble limbs when she came first
> To this bleak world; and she yet seemed to know
> On second sight her ancient playfellow, . . .
> (Hutchison 193)

In addition to Allegra's phantasm, Shelley also saw his own phantasm, as he walked on the veranda of his home. It spoke to him and asked him how long he meant to be content. Jane Williams, too, saw Shelley's phantasm twice, each time going in the same direction, an impossibility according to the construction of his home, while she was standing with Edward Trelawny, who did not see the phantasm. Shelley was reported to have been elsewhere at the time.

In one of his prophetic dreams just days before his death, Shelley was warned by Edward and Jane Williams that the sea was flooding their house. Whereupon, Shelley stood and saw "the sea rushing in". Was this the water which would flood into his boat, wherein he and Edward Williams would die? Was Shelley not like his Promethean hero, whose prescience and forethought, saw ahead into the unknown, to see the eventual known?

Shelley's projections and transferences into his art seem to mirror, in certain respects, some of the events and experiences of his last months of life. As poignant as these things are, parallels are also present in his beautiful and prophetic stanzas LIV and LV of *Adonais* written in eulogy of John Keats.

LIV
That Light whose smile kindles the Universe,
That Beauty in which all things work and move,
That Benediction which the eclipsing Curse
Of birth can quench not, that sustaining Love
Which through the web of being blindly wove
By man and beast and earth and air and sea,
Burns bright or dim, as each are mirrors of
The fire for which all thirst; now beams on me,
Consuming the last clouds of cold mortality.

LV
The breath whose might I have invoked in song
Descends on me; my spirit's bark is driven,
Far from the shore, far from the trembling throng
Whose sails were never to the tempest given;
The massy earth and sphered skies are riven!
I am born darkly, fearfully, afar;
Whilst burning through the inmost veil of Heaven,
The soul of Adonais, like a star,
Beacons from the abode where the Eternal are.
(441-442)

Shelley, thus, reveals a duality and complexity within the psyche with extrapsychic ramifications in his artistic creations and within himself. He joins his shadow, his phantasm, while first being drawn to "That Light . . . That Beauty . . . That Benediction . . . The fire for which all thirst . . . where the Eternal are."

CHARLES KINGSLEY'S SEA CHANGE: THE ALLEGORY OF THE *WATER BABIES*

> Who shall ascend into the hill of the Lord? or who shall stand in his holy place? He that hath clean hands, and a pure heart.
>
> —Psalms 3-4

One is delighted by Charles Kingsley's *Water Babies* just as one is delighted by the prodigiously humorous *Zoonomia* of Erasmus Darwin, the precursor of evolution and the grandfather of Charles Darwin. As Erasmus Darwin was a precursor of evolution, Charles Kingsley was an advocate and disperser of it:

> I have gradually learnt to see that it is just as noble a conception of Deity to believe that He created primal forms capable of self-development into all forms needful protempore and proloco, as to believe that He required a fresh act of intervention to supply the lacuna which He himself had made. I question whether the former be not the loftier view. (Fabian 287)

In fact, Kingsley took evolution back to the sea, clearly much further back than to the great apes. He seemed to be adding his bit of understanding to evolution, and as luck or prophecy would have it (he was a Victorian Apostle, after all), modern science seems to agree with his point, although Kingsley may have only meant it metaphorically in 1862 and 1863. Cyril Ponnamperuma,

President of the International Society for the Study of Life, has said (in 1986) that "the universe appears to me to be in the business of making life." Furthermore, Ponnanmperuma has stated:

> that a primitive ocean seemed to make the most sense as life's birthplace. The simplest explanation is that it happened in water. We should try to look for other explanations in the atmosphere and dust, if there was no water. But all the information we have points in that direction. As scientists, we can't rule out other possibilities, but those are not the most likely explanations. (McDonald 6-9)

With this in mind, the knowledge of the *Water Babies* seems somewhat prescient. The text of the *Water Babies* works as an allegory because its metaphors are stronger than extended metaphors. Tom's transformation has remarkable similarities to those within and of *Everyman* and a *Pilgrim's Progress*. It is difficult to consider Kingsley's book as a children's book, or a fairy tale, in the strictest senses, although children would and probably do enjoy this book for various reasons. It seems a story for mature souls as well as for those who are still developing, no matter at what age. The sense of "play" in the book and its more profound sense of wish fulfillment on the part of its author stand out strikingly. The book explicates many of Kingsley's social goals metaphorically, makes use of a hierarchic strategy which was indicative of some of his personality traits—especially his sense of whimsy, his sense of caring, and (most importantly) his provocative and prophetic imagination.

Charles Kingsley was a Renaissance man in the way that few Victorians could be, or few moderns for that matter. His many talents were not the only indicators for his Renaissance quality, however, but additional indicators were his richness of thought, feeling, and the bibliography from which he read. He was aware, and could accept the fact that although the Old and New Testaments might be inaccurate as historical records to some degree, they presented a higher kind of truth than that which he saw evinced in the social life of England of his day, and within the material quality of life of the working classes. With Frederick Denison Maurice, John Ludlow, Thomas Hughes, and Edward Vansittart Neale, Kingsley was a Christian Socialist and helped to form that society. These men formed the Christian Socialists as a pressure group:

> They had hoped to build a just and satisfying society, their kind of socialism, through work, example and education, awakening the middle class to their responsibilities and the working class to their potential. (Colloms 2)

Kingsley was also influenced by the Chartists; the Chartists were a working class group which had combined their efforts with some social agitators, and when the Christian Socialist newspaper was founded in late 1850, many Chartists contributed articles to the publication. Among a plethora of interests, Kingsley was also an amateur rock collector, an ardent examiner of seaside marine life, and discoverer with Sir John Lubbock of the fossilized remains of a musk-ox in a gravel pit in the Thames Valley (Huxley 264).

Thus, in 1863, he was made a fellow of the Geological Society. Sir Charles Burnbury, who was friends with Sir Charles Lyell and T. H. Huxley, was responsible for Kingsley's induction into the society. Bunbury said of Kingsley:

> He is truly a noble man. And the extent and variety of his knowledge are astonishing. He is not only an eloquent preacher and moralist, a poet and novelist, but an accomplished naturalist and antiquarian, an eager sportsman. What is he not? (Huxley 264)

Kingsley developed correspondences with both Charles Darwin and with T. H. Huxley. To Darwin he said that he had not known:

> that I could begin to study nature anew, now that you have made it to me a living thing, not a dead collection of means. But my work lies elsewhere now. Your work, nevertheless, helps mine at every turn. (Huxley 265-66)

Some of Kingsley's other interests, other than those already noted, included among them: public health, especially sanitation, girls' education, household suffrage, an extension of the Reform Bill, the Working Men's College, and the plights of children living by theft and prostitution. He felt that women were often superior to men "by reason of their greater sensitivity and capacity for tenderness and compassion" (Huxley 270-71). Thus, it is easy to agree with Bunbury that Kingsley's was, indeed, a noble nature and, in fact, a rare one.

Much that is good and helpful concerning the meanings of the *Water Babies* has already been written but does not discuss, however, the text with its criss-crossings of the Classical paradigmatic Zeus-Prometheus-Epimetheus-Fire allegory and the new Darwinian paradigmatic models within its covers. Most critics and biographers who have written about the book have often recapped and only indulged in plot summary. However, Larry Uffelman in his *Charles Kingsley* has tried to iterate part of the structural beauty of Kingsley's work. For instance, he has noted:

> In the *Water Babies* . . . Kingsley placed the nineteenth-century conflict between science and religion in the context of a fantasy designed to reconcile them by showing continuous development to be the creative principles of evolution in the physical world to the growth and maturity of the spiritual being . . . Victorian children, taught by Kingsley's fantasy, should see that an imaginative vision of the material world opens to them a spiritual reality not perceptible by the senses alone. These children should be able to accept the advances of science without losing their Christian faith. (Uffelman 71)

On the other hand, what is Christian in the book is clearly not obviously so, although there is within the text a blend of several Christian ideals; they are not specifically stated but often used allegorically. Too much literalness would have been too dogmatic for Kingsley, and too far from his many crucial, other points in the book. Too, Uffelman's notations on how Victorian children might respond to the book does not attempt to mention how other historical readers might react to the text.

Clearly, modern and postmodern readers might have gotten and get, respectively, just as much from this novel, and perhaps more because of the passage of time and the passing of many other important scientific and historic moments. Our horizon of expectations are not that great in spite of the leaps within the scientific community since that time, as the fiction itself pointed to profound changes. Although the book is a fantasy, as noted, it is more of a phantasmagoria or a psychomachia in breadth. It is, in other words, complex, and perhaps not just "one thing" as much as a variety of things, including an early version of pastiche. Uffelman did not note how Kingsley dealt with his interests in sanitation and education in this text, nor, indeed, how Kingsley accomplishes the reconciliation of the sciences with religion, although one writer cannot cover everything in explication with so many other details to attend to in a biography. Yet, Kingsley's interests in trans-class striving are also important within the narrative.

After all, Tom, his textual hero and primary character, goes from being a lower-class chimney sweep, at the beginning of the book, to a man of science by the end of it. On the other hand, because Tom is part of a "fairy tale" (as Kingsley denotes his text), Tom and Ellie are not allowed to marry:

> Don't you know that no one ever marries in a fairy tale, under the rank of a prince or a princess? (Fabian 385)

We are not sure whether this is some ultimate snobbery on the part of Kingsley, or a subtle poke at the monarchy. For the seeming eternity of this "fairy tale" which has extraordinary allegorical underpinnings, Tom is only allowed to visit Ellie on Sundays (perhaps the Victorian influence to the fairy tale), even though Kingsley made it clear to his readers that Tom and Ellie were very much in love; they both grew separately as individuals. Ellie changed from the screaming young lady of the beginning to a daring and enamored young lady at the end of the text. Perhaps Kingsley's ending is, in fact, an oblique invitation to his Victorian readers to go beyond "Sunday" meetings, especially in similar kinds of circumstances of social growth and personal maturation on the parts of "real" protagonists in non-fairy-tale adventures.

Tom is transformed from a little boy to a sea creature in Kingsley's book. He is changed from a dirty chimney sweep because of the "cleanliness" of his seeming "eternal" presence in the stream and the sea. Too, there he has stopped being a young rascal of no ambition by being educated to the "wonders" of the world beneath the water. Kingsley and the fairies even rid Tom of the victimization he had endured through the perturbations of the grimy Mr. Grimes. The fairies first killed Grimes, or helped him to get his due, and even though he becomes literally clean in the sea, he is, or becomes, instead of supervisor of chimney sweeps, the eternity-long chimney sweep of Mount Etna, out of harms way to little children.

The fairies fulfill a dual function. Syncretically, they are both pagan, as allegorical representatives of the fairy world and Christian, finally, in terms of their behavior, representing as they do the "ideal" of goodness and poetic justice. Kingsley, through them, in two instances, uses the Christian eulogy of "Do unto others as you would have them do unto you" to create two allegorical and personified characters who are, until a fateful time in the future of the text, binary opposites as well. These two are Mrs. Bedonebyasyoudid and Mrs. Doasyouwouldbedoneby.

In continuing Kingsley's Christian theme, Tom's transformation as well as being a new life unto Christ or a metaphor for being "born again," is a socially significant kind of allegorical statement. It could happen to anyone, Kingsley might be saying, even without the intervention of fairies, rites-of-passage being what they are in all of our lives. The idea of changing classes or even of changing one's class values, for those of another, are significant issues, even a bit revolutionary (a 360-degree turn) for a Victorian, no matter who or what the aegis of intervention to promote such changes. Importantly, too, are the inherent ideas of the text that one can overcome one's victimizers, that one can change one's life status, and Kingsley's clarity of judgment that indicates that Tom's quality is greater and more valuable than that of the brutal Grimes. Tom is the innocent, in spite of his own grime, when he falls all unwittingly into the clean "white" paradise-like room of Ellie while trying to clean the chimney of her parents' home.

A real concern for the welfare of Kingsley's own children is one of the vibrant echoes of the text; children need concerned and vital educators to be dedicated and aware enough to try to help them through the troublesome and, yet, potentially exotic world. Children need to see the beauty and complexity of the world, even its subterranean aspects, as well as to be conscious of its limitations and difficulties. Through the experience of beauty, as in Tom's "underworld" and underwater sea-odyssey, which the book depicts (mirroring Kingsley's personal interest in examining seaside marine life), specific options and potentialities have been developed for children.

One of the underlying and cogent premises of the book is that as the horizons of children are expanded, so, too, will be their future life experiences. Kingsley metaphorically provides the notion that children need diversity and options provided for them. These are the interesting and optimistic sentiments within the text, as well as the demanding ones. This sense of responsibility to and for children which the fairies assume, is both a very maternal and paternal vision, one with which Kingsley felt comfortable. His text, written for a new son, clearly was an indication of Kingsley's commitment to his son as well as a parable for the sons and daughters, and their parents, of his readers.

Besides being aware of the book's moral overtones (and undertows, as undertones) readers may become fascinated by Kingsley's structural constructs. His uses of horizontals and verticals are noteworthy. For instance, Tom must go "backwards" to a more primitive state in evolution (biologically, psychologically, and socially) in order to "find" himself and his way out (beyond "The

Other End of Nowhere," one of the names of the chapters of the book, in this utopian abridgment of childhood) to reality, as well as to earlier having gone "up and down" within chimneys, "down" and "under" water (to swim horizontally like a fish, to experience diverse forms of life, instead of standing vertically) in both the local stream and the larger ocean, eventually to "rise" above this important fall, within creation, (most commonly referred to as a learning experience) to climb, anew, both literally and figuratively to a new vertical stance, with refreshed and refined vision. Kingsley, in homage to his own strivings and to those of many of his friends, privileges the position of "scientist" within the book by allowing Tom to become one.

It was from Mother *Carey* (she cares) that Tom first learned of the pragmatic pagan Epimetheus (he is privileged first by Kingsley in this allegory), of his wife Pandora, and of his brother Prometheus, the highly touted prescient-sensed being who also endured "long-suffering" for his vision and committed stance. However, Zeus is interestingly missing from the remnants of the telling of the allegorical pantheon, which itself is told near the end of Kingsley's tale and in a fragmented form (which may be why "Afterthought" is mentioned first because the textual addition of the pantheon by Kingsley seems to be an afterthought). Still one senses the importance of this remnant within the structure of the text. Kingsley was clearly in favor of the prescient sensibility, as he seemed to have some of it, but he was not in favor of long-suffering unless the rewards of the suffering were related to new knowledge and growth. Thus, in his text, he links the pagan, aspects of evolution, and Christian understanding. His is the first text with such overall links to the past and the present wherein these elements are intertwined for reformulation and rethinking intertextually for readers of fiction. Thus, too, are the paradigms imploded upon one another. Going into the pantheon, the outer limits of the earth and sky, is no longer the only way to understand humanity, thanks to Erasmus and Charles Darwin, and to Kingsley's interest and belief in their work.

Kingsley's kindness of thought and breadth of vision to use these paradigmatic remnants can help us to appreciate the kind part of humankind, in a way in which we might not have been able to do without his *Water Babies* production. One respects his kind of thinker, not only because he is rare, but because somewhere in this atomistic universe, within the cosmos or beyond a red limit, perhaps not in the heaven which Kingsley or others of us so anthropomorphically and allegorically conceive, is the sense of a stature, presence or essence which glows so brightly as within our remembering sensibilities and imaginations with remarkably "clean hands" and a remarkably "pure heart" however that might be conceived in an "other silent speak"—perhaps a molecular one. To change, Kingsley indicates, is after all, to accept a challenge offered by earth, wind, fire, sea, sand, and stars. Nature beckons and human nature responds miraculously at times; if we could respond positively instead of negatively, like our projected Prometheus or our seemingly more simple cousin, the chimpanzee, our earth might be a cleaner and purer place.

It will be Edgar Rice Burroughs in his *Tarzan of the Apes* and Robert Louis Stevenson in his *Dr. Jekyl and Mr. Hyde* who will bring the more furry, forested aspect of evolution to cognition for consideration, up from Kingsley's sea change. Kingsley, Burroughs, and Stevenson have helped us to go beyond human dreams of the "out there" (as gods and goddesses) to our realities of down here, to more human and monkey-like, symbolically/metaphorically (or literally) biological qualities. It will be Charles Lumsden and Edward O. Wilson in their *Promethean Fire: Reflections on the Origin of Mind* who will relink gods, apes, and our ancient ancestors in their biopsychological text. Hopefully, we can now enjoy the varied explication of all of our transformations and metamorphoses, symbolical or otherwise. If we can accept all aspects of our humanhood, from the highest to the lowest, perhaps our evolutions will not have been in vain as it sometimes does seem, and humankind will have grown from the sea babies that we were, as well as from the gods and goddesses that we had wished to be. Perhaps,

Promethean like, we can still be positive about human-kind, and be kinder about that potential "ape" within as well, accepting the fire of insight about its potential figuratively.

VII

ROBERT BRIDGES AND HIS
PROMETHEUS THE FIREGIVER:
CLOSE READING AND EXPLICATION

Robert Bridges' *Prometheus the Firegiver* is a distinguished poetic Mask concerning the subjects of Prometheus, Zeus, and by inference "fire", which at some points in the narrative take on the significance of character. Bridges had the solid backing of his government, and even though he turned down the Professorship of Poetry at Oxford University in 1895, he was, nonetheless, made poet laureate of Britain in 1913. He also received the Order of Merit, in 1929, for his book *The Testament of Beauty*, in which he noted of beauty:

> Beauty is the highest of all those occult influences.
> the quality of appearance that thru the sense
> wakeneth spiritual emotion in the mind of man.
> (Dobree 7)

His interest in beauty is an aesthetic which is apparent in his *Prometheus the Firegiver* as well; it is an aesthetic which posits Prometheus foremost as a giver and not as a thief.

Bridges, forced by illness, retired from medical practice in 1881. He then became a poet only when his "muse" attended him, but was also an essayist (*Collected Essays and Papers*, 10 vols.), a literary critic, an editor (his own work and *Poems of Gerard Manley Hopkins*), one of the founders (with Henry Bradley, Sir Walter Raleigh, and Logan Pearsall Smith) in 1913 of the Society of Pure

English, and something of a linguist in that he devised an ingenious and elaborate phonetic typography (Dobree 17). As a friend of Gerard Manley Hopkins, he helped start Hopkins' career by publishing five of his poems in his book *The Spirit of Man*. Also a friend of W. B. Yeats, Yeats had said of Bridges:

> His influence—practice not theory—was never deadening; he gave to lyric poetry a new cadence, a distinction as deliberate as that of Whistler's painting, an impulse moulded and checked like that in certain poems of Landor, but different, more with nerves, less in the blood, more birdlike, less human; words often commonplace made unforgettable by some trick of speeding and slowing,
>
>> A glitter of pleasure
>> And a dark tomb,
>
> or by some trick of simplicity, not the impulsive simplicity of youth but that of age, much impulse examined and rejected. (Sparrow 1955)

Bridges, who also enjoyed archaisms in language, using them freely and with pleasure, mastered metaphor. Bridges, or the persona of his poem, allows himself to become a bird in his untitled poem:

> I would be a bird, and straight on wings I arise,
> And carry purpose up to the ends of air:
> In calm and storm my sails I feather, and where
> By breezing cliffs the unransomed wreckage lies:
> Or strutting on hot meridian banks, surprise
> The silence: over plains on the moonlight bare
> I chase my shadow and perch where no bird dare
> In treetops torn by fiercest winds of the skies.
> Poor simple birds, foolish birds! then I cry,
> Ye pretty pictures of delight, unstirred
> By the only joy of knowing that ye fly,
> Ye are not what ye are, but rather, sum'd on
>> a word,
> The alphabet of a god's idea, and I
> Who master it, I am the only bird. (Dobree 31)

And, although, Gerard Manley Hopkins once suggested that Bridges was too "pagan" for him, he, nonetheless, saved all the letters that Bridges ever wrote to him. It is to the master of "the alphabet of a god's idea," the pagan, to this bird of the possible metaphor, that one must turn in order to review how Bridges used flame imagery, the flame as metaphor, and his abacus of the Zeus-Prometheus-Epimetheus-Fire paradigm in *Prometheus the Firegiver*. Just by his title, the reader notes that Prometheus has been favored with primary attention (or allegorically his kind of thought reigned, not that that was his object); and, in that sense, he has achieved the kingship of the monarchy of the pantheon within the minds of authors perceiving him. He achieved this pinnacle slowly within the minds of the authors who chose to ponder his fictive development, and to write their intentions.

However, in one exquisite section of a verse from an untitled poem (first line: "My delight and thy delight"), Bridges captured one of the sensual resonances which the flame image has come to connote:

> My desire and thy desire
> Twining to a tongue of fire,
> Leeping live, and laughing higher;
> Thro' the everlasting strife
> In the mystery of life. (19)

Also, one part of the *Ode* which ends *Prometheus the Firegiver* was published in 1890 as an untitled poem in *The Shorter Poems of Robert Bridges* and in 1914 in *Bridges Poetical Works*:

> Book III, I
>   O my vague desires!
> Ye lambent flames of the soul, her offspring fires:
> That are my soul herself in pangs sublime
> Rising and flying to heaven before her time:
>   What doth tempt you forth
> To drown in the south or shiver in the frosty north?
> What seek ye or find ye in your random flying,
> Ever roaring aloft, soaring and dying?
>   Joy, the joy of flight!
> They hide in the sun, they flare and dance in the night;

> Gone up, gone out of sights: and ever again
> Follow fresh tongues of fire, fresh pangs of pain.
>
>   Ah! they burn my soul,
> The fires, devour my soul that once was whole:
> She is scattered in fiery phantoms day by day,
> But whither, whither? ay whither? away, away?
>
>   Could I but control
> These vague desires, those leaping flames of the soul:
> Could I but quench the fire: ah! could I stay
> My soul that flieth, alas, and dieth away.
> (Bridges 264)

This poem, when read out of the context of its Promethean text, seems decidedly unPlatonic, as the soul is mortal. Within the text proper, however, that which is immortal is reason, the reason of humankind. But within the poem or ode, in whichever version it is read, fire is a metaphor for the soul, and seems to be a persona, just as the "vague desires" are. The "flames of the soul" and "her offspring fires" have lives of their own, as soul. They leave the corporeal body (of the persona), dying and being reborn and reborn, over and over again, flying. Then, the fires of the soul disperse the soul, in a kind of expansion, like atoms outward, until evaporation, and death. This kind of "evaporation" within the Mask may be an identification with Prometheus who seems to evaporate when he disappears in the final scene.

What made Robert Bridges' poetry and Robert Bridges the man all the more remarkable, however, were the early recognitions of his double interests in both medicine and poetry, seeming to reveal his pragmatic and nonpragmatic sensibilities. He decided to become a doctor first, and hoped to begin a career in poetry after his career in medicine. From 1869-1874, he was a student of medicine at St. Bartholomew's, receiving his M.B. in 1874. In 1881, a serious illness forced him to abandon medical practice, as noted earlier. In 1882, he completed, at Yattendon, his country home, his first poetic piece which was to be published privately in 1883 (Sparrow). As a High Anglican, and in spite of Hopkin's charge of Bridges' paganism, it seems inevitable that Christianity influenced aspects of his play, structurally and syncretically. For no matter how "pagan" he seemed, this melodic syncretism is obvious in his first work, with pagan and Christian morals intertwining.

Bridges' Prometheus was a powerful expression of Hesiod's paradigm, but a character imaginatively recreated anew in the mind of Bridges. The plot of Bridges' mask is a remarkable departure from the previous works cited. Bridges' text is a compendium of many aspects of the other retold tales of Prometheus, but, within this text, Prometheus allegorically became part of the established order of ritual, belief, and worship on earth; his kind of thought dominated. As a giver of fire, Prometheus herein, textually, assumed his godhead for personkind *before* he had to pay any penalty or punishment to Zeus. He assumed this godhead because he was a greater advocate to the progress of humanity.

Too, in his daring plot, Bridges draws the Io story from Aeschylus, expanding it, and drawing in Inachus and Argeia, her parents, as characters. Zeus was replaced completely because he had rejected any responsibility for humans completely. Bridges portrays Prometheus as totally committed to Homo sapiens, seeming Christ-like, and interacting with humans, rather than suffering in the Caucasus.

In the opening scene, Prometheus mentioned that Zeus was one who was "angry" and one who "bends the wills of gods." Prometheus, it is obvious does not want to be bent or to bend the will of those of his greatest desire—humans. Earth for Prometheus was

> . . . this nether world
> My truant haunt is . . . (Bridges ll. 8-9)

He steals to earth from Olympus. He likes earth because on earth he can taste "the mortal joy". None among the gods, except Prometheus, had:

> A touch so keen, to wake such love of life
> As stirs the frail and careful being, who here,
> The king of sorrows, melancholy man,
> Bows at his labour, but in heart erect
> A god stands, nor for any gift of god
> Would barter his immortal hearted prime. (ll. 19-24)

The human, for Bridges, has a Promethean heart. Prometheus longed to roam earth because he loved humanity. For this love, Zeus would have destroyed Prometheus because he feared for his own demise and replacement.

Zeus used Prometheus' counseling in deposing the Titans and, afterward he became elevated to the highest godhead. Zeus became over-confident and began to ignore Prometheus' counseling. Zeus wanted to remake everything in the universe anew, displaying to Prometheus a nature ". . . wanton, as a youth first tasting power" (1.47). Zeus, too, was "Determined to destroy the race of men, /And that create afresh or else have none" (ll. 51-52). Thus, Bridges interpreted and expanded the context for the characters beyond what Hesiod presented.

Zeus tried to destroy the earth in floods. Just as Deucalion and Noah survived their floods, so there were those humans, prewarned by Prometheus, who survived Zeus' floods. Seeing the human survivors, Zeus then decided to withdraw "the seeds of fire" from "withered branch and the blue flakes of flint". With these things withdrawn, man becomes "with the brutes degraded". It is this struggle to separate humans with malice and bully-like reason, from other living creatures, which concerns Bridges for the rest of his play. Bridges' explication for personkind, textually, insures that they must take responsibility for their behavioral acts, their knowledge, and their need to be altruistic, to help others, just as Bridges did in his personal life through medicine and writing. His text reflects his own values. Prometheus, too,

> . . . upheld
> The weak and pitying them sent sweet Hope,
> Bearer of dreams, enchantress fond and kind,
> From heaven descending on the unhindered rays
> Of every star . . . (ll. 74-78)

by bringing a "prisoner" which was

> . . . stolen from heaven
> the flash of mastering fire . . .
> For man the father of all fire to come. (ll. 82-84)

Being "father of all fire to come" brings with it inherent

responsibilities to tend to the positive aspects of fire, not the destructive ignorance of it and its hazardous potential.

Bridges' Prometheus, the "enlightened representative of mind" on the allegorical level, chose to give fire to Inachus because Inachus "was hopeful, careful, wise and brave." And like Deucalion and Noah, it was Inachus who helped to restore humans from another flood, to reorganize, and to "live not brutally though without fire." Inachus assumed "guilt" for the withholding of fire by Zeus, wrongly, showing a kind of innate masochism, mental bondage to tyranny, and even an inverted presumption. Zeus is a fierce superego figure (over I) for Inachus, too, whom is only child-like waiting for an idealized good mother or father help. Inachus' behavior of continuing to offer sacrifices to Zeus was what Prometheus wished to stop, because he saw its pathos; he knew that: "All is not good for man that seems god's will." Prometheus, though not revealing his identity, appeared to one of Inachus' servants at the site of the sacrifice. While trying to compare Zeus to Inachus, Inachus arrived on the scene with his chorus and his semichorus as attendants. In trying to purge the site of any impure elements, Inachus incited Prometheus to speak out, and invited his semichorus to divulge information concerning a gift of a sacred tree "with apples gold thereon" for Hera. Hera was informed and she was delighted. She found the tree in a garden, fenced with groves around:

> Nature had kissed Art
> And born a child to stir
> With jealousy the heart
> of heavens Artificer. (ll. 309-312)

This garden is syncretically like Eden, yet with a tree of golden apples. Instead of bringing destruction to humans, the tree is a symbol of artistic creation, a specific kind of power to allow the upset of Zeus, by provocation in attracting his wife, if by no other means. Prometheus (with all of his foreknowledge) had thought ahead as usual, and before he spoke against Zeus, he first spoke in favor of Inachus, stating that Inachus' fame had reached far:

> . . . men
> That ne'er have seen thee tell that
> thou art set
> Upon the throne of virtue, that
> good-will
> And love thy servants are, that in thy land
> joy, honour, truth and modesty abide
> And drink the air of peace, that
> kings must see.
> Thy city, would they know their
> peoples good
> And stablish them therein by wholesome laws.
> (ll. 334-341)

Prometheus is all aware of the strange psychomachia going on within Inachus and aware, too, of his weak ego and mind state as he asked:

> Hast thou not proved and found the will of Zeus
> A barren rock for man with prayer to plow?
> (ll. 396-397)

Bridge's Prometheus, in encouraging Inachus, through Bridges' re-use of this theme, wanted Inachus to know that he would suffer when he saw the truth because he had held back for so long before accepting fire. His logic was continued as he told Inachus that to incur the wrath of Zeus, as he himself had done (either as internal {intrapsychic} superego, external fascist, tyrant, or negative parent figure) was a necessity for human need and desire for fire both literally and figuratively:

> . . . is the unquenchable
> original cause, the immortal breath of being:
> Nor is there any spirit on Earth astir,
> Nor 'neath the airy vault nor yet beyond
> In any dweller in far-reaching space
> Nobler or dearer than the spirit of man:
> That spirit which lives in each and will not die,
> That wooeth beauty, and for all good things
> Urgeth a voice, or still in passion fighteth
> And where he loveth draweth the heart with him.
> (ll. 461-470)

Prometheus rather insisted that Inachus listen to his own internal spirit for justifiable reasons which would lead to insight for Inachus, and possibly for others through his example:

> . . . O hark to him!
> For else if folly shut his joyous strength
> To mope in her dark prison without praise,
> The hidden tears with which he wails his wrong
> Will sour the fount of life. O hark to Him!
> Him may'st thou trust beyond the things thou seest.
> For many things there be upon this earth
> Unblest and fallen from beauty, to mislead
> Man's mind, and in a shadow justify
> The evil thoughts and deeds that work his ill.
> Fear, hatred, lust and strife, which if man question
> The heaven born spirit within him, are not there.
> (ll. 474-485)

Prometheus has what Bridges calls a "manlike spirit" and knows that humankind is better than tyrannical force (whether experienced extrapsychically or intrapsychically) because humans have:

> . . . more power for good than Zeus for ill
> More courage, justice, more abundant art,
> More love, more joy, more reason: though around thee
> Rank-rooting evil bloom with poisonous crown, . . .
> (ll. 497-500)

Inachus, listening intently to all of this, began to change inwardly, and responded to Prometheus that he wanted fire for future generations to provide "barest needs".

> . . . Nature in recovering her right
> Would kinder prove to man who seeks to learn
> Her secrets and unfold the cause of life.
> So tell me, if thou knowest, what is fire! (ll. 521–534)

Fire, thus, enters the speculative world of Bridges' Mask, upon the stage of philosophical inquiry within a definitive world of words, as part of the extension of Hesiod's wisdom literature. Prometheus thrilled at this response:

> Thy wish to know is good, and happy is he
> Who thus from chance and change has launched his
> mind
> To dwell with undisturbed truth. (ll. 536-539)

Learning, then, according to Bridges' Prometheus, required a flexible mind, one which is capable of inquiry and potential change after the inquiries are made. Acknowledging that one is willing to change both opinion and behavior after inquiry is to acknowledge, before that actuality, this possibility—linking individuals closer to foreknowledge, or a kind of "advance" knowing. Therefore, one becomes more Promethean like, as the critic Denis Donoghue had hoped for and speculated upon in his *Thieves of Fire*.

However, Prometheus tried to tell this "truth" of fire with an allegorical story, which can be seen as having a parable-like quality in order to respond to Inachus' question. He, therefore, described fire as a "raging power" which had been decreed a slow diminishing "old age". The personified Fire bequeathed this power to his daughter, "the Queen of clear and azure Firmament"—Air. When Air took her inheritance, "the one-mooned earth" was a sheet of flame, like the sun. Air tempered this flame into the earth

> . . . in dens and bowels
> of earth to smoulder . . . (ll. 605-606)

She brought, then, to earth water, pools, and seas:

> . . . from whence she drew the fertile seeds
> Of trees and plants, and last of footed life
> . . . (ll. 612-613)

Air predated *Genesis* and the patriarchal aspect of that text with her gender identification. This is a link to Kingsley's sea as being the originator of life, but with the prime mover of plant and other life being Air. Reason, whose genealogy we are not given by Bridges, praised the work of Air; Air, pleased, asked a favor of Reason:

Make thou one fair thing for me which will suit
With what is made, and be the best of all.
'Twas evening, and that night Reason made man. (ll.
620-622)

Air, though, as the child of Fire was destined to die. To
this knowledge the semichorus, after hearing Prometheus'
parable, responded:

Maidens: Children of *air* are we, and live by *fire*.
Youth: The sons of Reason dwelling on Earth.
Maidens: Folk of a pleasant kingdom held between
         Fire's reign of terror and the latter day
         When dying soon in turn his child must
         die.
Youth: Having a wise creator, above time
         Or youth or change, from who our kind
         inherit
         The grace and pleasure of the eternal gods.
         (ll. 623-630)

This important, and what appears to be critically ignored
text links the gods with the personified elements of Fire
and Air, and finally with mortals whom inherit "The grace
and pleasure of the eternal gods" though not their
eternality. Interestingly within Bridges' text, he replaces
in lower-case initial letters the words air and fire, which
are clone-like imitations of the raging power "Fire" and
his daughter "Air"—the abstractions and personifications
of forces replacing them in a literal context on earth,
breathing air, and using fire to live. The repetition is part
of the ritualization of the ideas, and part of the need to
have the figurative allegory linked to the literal. The explication that there is a "dying time" for everything but
the "eternal gods" and the "wise creator" Reason. Thus
are Reason and the gods linked into eternity. The human race is the inheritor of reason and linked, thus, to
immortality.

Within Bridges' work, there is a strong egalitarian
sensibility expressed within the parable, in which the
parallel structures need examination. The personified Fire
and Air die (corporeally), but the gods do not. Humans
die (corporeally) as does the soul, but Reason (the wise

creator) implants an inheritance within humans which does not die. There is an equation of the "gods" with the "reason" of personkind as being eternal. Reason is eternal and noncorporeal. If it was our reason which projected gods as a method of learning and explicating identity and consciousness, then Bridges' clever explication through his poetic play links human beings with the eternal, in spite of our corporeal destiny, as members of both an evolutionary and spiritual order.

Textually, after Prometheus had told Inachus this parable, he was still too frightened to take fire from Prometheus because he still feared Zeus' wrath, but only temporarily. Finally, he was able to take fire from Prometheus and to accept responsibility for governing insight and specific kinds of knowledge (metaphors for fire).

Prometheus the "prophet," the foreknower, had helped Zeus with the Titans, but now he helps humans. For with fire will be given:

> The cunning of invention and all the arts
> In which thy hand, instructed may command,
> Interpret, comfort or ennoble nature,
> With all provision that in wisdom is,
> And what prevention in foreknowledge lies.
> (ll. 696-700)

In accepting the gifts of Prometheus, Inachus not only accepted the responsibility for his action, but the freedom which came with it; so he no longer would be

> . . . a harnessed brute,
> Flogged to his daily work, that cannot view
> The high design to which his labor steps
> . . . (ll. 709-711)

and, too, when he dies, he will:

> . . . from the tomb go forth a flame. (l. 726)

Here, again, the reader can view Bridges' powerful, evocative use of metaphor in his text, and his profound understanding of both allegory and metaphor. He plays with

Hesiod's text, culling deeply the psychology behind the original skeletal construct. Too, the reader notes that for Bridges, unlike Plato's "soul," reason is the purest and most everlasting form of existence and expression. Since reason is linked in metaphoric association with fire, which as an element must die, it lives ethereally, both in absence and in literal presence, in the intelligence of humans. One becomes the other, and then again becomes the other, into linked transformations.

Too, returning to the drama, the final acceptance by Inachus pleased Prometheus, because without humanity acting as a gardener, nature would be a "desert wild." Hominid shall imagine or "picture what will be" in assuming an identity with the Promethean mind, foreknowledge. Too, those who see the

>   . . . face
> And form of beauty . . . (ll. 766-767)

shall be nature's "heart and life", born

>   . . . to shield
> A happier birthright with intrepid arms,
> To tread down tyranny and fashion forth
> A virgin wisdom to subject the world,
> To build for passion an eternal song,
> To shape her dreams in marble, and so sweet
> Their speech, that envious Time hearkening shall stay
> In fear to snatch, and hide his rugged hand.
> Now is the birthday of thy conquering youth.
> O man, and lo thy priest and prophet stand
> Before the altar and have blessed the day.
> (ll. 668-678)

Prometheus, representative of a special kind of thought, marks himself as priest and prophet. He is an abstraction yet a corporeal presence. When asked by Inachus "Where is thy fire?" (1.779)—Prometheus answered "This was my message, speak and there is fire" (1. 781). Later, Inachus will note after the disappearance of Prometheus from the scene and presumably from the earth:

. . . and with his fire
Hath lit our sacrifice unto himself. (ll. 1392-1393)

He has, therefore, within the logos and before his punishment on the mighty rock in the Caucasus, given fire
through reasoning with men and women. Too, he has
replaced Zeus, and his name is placed over the altar
before he leaves. Fire is thus linked through language,
and reason, to the eternal, too.

The audience is introduced to both Argeia and Io,
wife and daughter to Inachus, respectively. Prometheus
and Inachus hear Argeia's fears for her children should
Inachus accept fire from Prometheus, and Inachus responds:

O deem not a man's children but those
Out of his loins engendered—our spirit's love
Hath such prolific consequence that virtue
Cometh of ancestry more pure than blood,
And counts her sand as seed upon the shore.
Happy is he whose body's sons proclaim
Their father's honour, but more blest to whom
The world is dutiful, whose children spring
Out of all nations, and whose pride the proud
Rise to regenerate when they call him sire. (ll. 988-
997).

Herein, Bridges expands responsibility to all children
sprung "out of all nations". Prometheus suggests that
those are more blest who are engendered from "spirit's
love" instead of genetically conceived. Thus, Fire, the
raging power, is now fire for the hearth, realms of labor,
the artistic, the mystic, and, allegorically, linked to the
responsibility for children. Controlling fire for constructive ends seems to be part of the semiotic of the text.
Too, the family of the world, an international configura-
tion, is finally of importance greater than the local family, ultimately, although both are important and worthy
of honor.

Prometheus had further calmed Argeia's fears, as-
suring her that foreknowledge would not be harmful to
individuals nor would it deviate their "motions." Further,
in telling Argeia of the fate of her daughter, Io, another
revelation is made. Io would wander the earth as a cow,

goaded by a "venomous fly" until she would hear Prometheus as:

> . . . a far-off cry,
> Whose throat seems the white mountain and its
>   passion
> The woe of earth. Flee not, nor turn back:
> Let thine ears drink and guide thine eyes to see
> That sight whose terrors shall assuage thy terror,
> Whose pains shall kill thy pain stretched on the rock,
> Naked to scorching sun, to pinching frost,
> To wind and storm and beaks of winged fiends.
> From year to year he lies. Refrain to ask
> His name and crime—nay, haply when thou seek him
> Thou wilt remember—tis thy tyrant's foe,
> Man's friend, who pays his chosen penalty.
> Draw near my child, for he will know thy need,
> And point from land to land thy further path.
> (ll. 1158-1171)

Womankind is linked here to the revelation of reason through Prometheus, that which is eternal and undying. Womankind will be freed from the "dumbness" of the curse of an unreasoning mind of a cow, and will go, ultimately, forward with her "need" fulfilled with instruction. Too, in Hesiod, she is the prophet of Promethean liberation; when many generations removed, her genetic ancestor; Hercules, will free him. Furthering the link between the two, is Inachus, who will rename Prometheus as "Io Prometheus" (l. 1394) for his *daughter*, after Prometheus disappears from the scene. Inachus states after this disappearance:

> And he, he now is gone; his work is done:
> 'Tis ours to see it be not done in vain. (ll. 1402-1403)

The catharsis related to Promethean rage and Promethean fire, and ultimate sacrifice, is the liberation of all. For in understanding the different kinds of thought, breaking Zeus down into his various allegorical parts, frees us to our responsibilities for all of our different kinds of thought and the thinking process itself. The ambivalent and arbitrary aspect which Zeus' name implies shall be no more.

In fact, Bridges replaces Zeus altogether: Through a section from his Chorus, he states that:

> . . . and now
> Seeing his altar is no more to Zeus,
> But shall ever be with smouldering heat
> Fed for the god who first set fire thereon,
> Change ye your hymns, which in the praise of Zeus
> Ye came to sing, and change the prayer for fire
> Which ye were wont to raise, to high thanksgiving,
> Praising aloud the giver and his gift. (ll. 1413-1420)

This poetic Mask marked Bridges' entrance into the poetic world. He chose this didactic theme, elaborated upon it, and created something wholly different from what Hesiod presented. He acknowledged in his text that the letters of Prometheus' name gave the "shape and soul to knowledge" (l. 1378). He even developed an explanation of Zeus's motive for the final punishment of Prometheus in a reasoned way. Not only was Bridges the metaphoric bird, but a metaphoric god, whose reason lived on after him within the potentially eternal corpus of his text.

Bridges' Victorian Prometheus is one of the last texts dealing fully with this theme. Prometheus, whose shadow had already crossed with Darwin's, would ever afterward be somehow diminished and dispelled; even as Io had gone on, we readers have turned our ways away from his suffering to his final victory. James Joyce, modernist extraordinary, will minimalize him but keep him intricately interwoven (but still burning), in other texts.

KINDLED FIRES IN *STEPHEN HERO,*
A PORTRAIT OF THE ARTIST AS A
YOUNG MAN, AND *ULYSSES*

Modernist literary and cinematic works stress vision
as a privileged mode of perception, even of revelation,
while at the same time cultivating opacity and questioning the primacy of the visible world. Furthermore,
the quest for autonomously generated, medium specific works results inversely in a serial pattern of
acknowledgements of (a) the ineluctable traces of the
picturing process in language and of (b) both the tendency to respond with linguistic and representational
reflexes to visual abstraction. One fascinating dimen-
sion of modernism is its apparent need to keep re-
producing allegories of these fundamental antimonies.
—P. Adams Sitney (from *Modernist Montage*)

The nature of the Promethean character is found metaphorically and most assuredly within the allegorical natures of both Stephen Dedalus and Leopold Bloom within
Ulysses as they have been developed by James Joyce.
They are both a reflection of the Promethean nature of
James Joyce. They are not only like Odysseus and
Telemachus structurally, as a prototype for father and
son reuniting, they are, too, by Joyce's use of symbolic
fire within his chapter "Ithaca" a link to a further distant mythic past than that of *The Odyssey,* to their earliest Greek religious significations. Unlike Mary Shelley's
Victor and his son, II, they are giving love to one another, and helping each other through significant social
rights of passage. Stephen allows himself to be a surro-

gate son for Bloom, and Bloom through transference and projection allows his love for Rudy to be rekindled, again, in his affection for Stephen. All is not lost for either of them.

Too, both men are searching heroically, in the ancient sense and psychologically in a modern sense, for self discovery within *Ulysses*. They want to know, whether consciously or not, and to understand themselves in a world in which they seem to have both lost their individual ways, much like Odysseus—a world which seems incomprehensible, painful, overwhelming in its natural aspects, seemingly on occasion magical and fantastic. Stephen in *Ulysses* in the chapter called "Scylla and Charybdis" is portrayed as being obsessed not only with Homer but with Shakespeare, too. Stephen successfully links Shakespeare's life to Shakespeare's works, creating a seeming musical medley.

Yet, the reader realizes that the art and the artist, no matter how strong their identifications (as Joyce with the Dedalus pseudonym before the Dedalus characterization) or their verisimilitude of characterization, are separate entities. (Perhaps, as in the choice of title of this chapter, one monster or the other from the symbolic consciousness is forever showing up when least expected.) The art is, as a part of the repository of gifts to humankind (for the artists and lovers of art therein), to do with as humankind can or will—to make of the work of art myriad understandings (which may or may not be related, historically). Art does not have to be a new revelation or new within the corpus; it can be a new twist on the old, or a pastiche. The artist's identification (personality) or creation may be a repository for him or her experience unto a wholly private experience of life, most probably comprehensible or accessible within the experience of the living of that life—unavailable for public consumption. This is part of the beauty of the legacy that James Joyce has left for us. The reader can appreciate the sovereignty of the art and the artist, because the demarcation of the domain is made explicit in the narrative and through the workings of symbols. In spite of all that, and ironically, there are moments when we honestly believe that the two are one, or like to think so—though in a flash the mirage is gone. So though Stephen is not James and vice-versa, the linkage of Stephen and Leopold, by contrast, is more striking for readers. The autobiography of James Joyce is deployed for these other means.

Stephen, then, in his explications concerning Shakespeare, is also explaining himself to us. Stephen like any god in any creation myth, pagan, Judaic, or Judeo-Christian is attempting to order the universe of his own existence as Joyce gave it to us in the *Portrait of the Artist as a Young Man*. Stephen at other times is trying to disorder the universe, exposing a side of his character too, nonetheless. But Stephen attempts to compress the fragments from the chaos and order of his own childhood and emerging boyhood in the early chapters of the *Portrait* all along the way and into *Ulysses*. How could a child who sees "this moocow that was coming down along the road met a nicens little boy named baby tuckoo . . ." grow up into an assimilated human being integrating a Mommy and a Dante, a Daddy and a Parnell, to name a few of the bare bones? Indeed, how could anyone? James Joyce lets us know that the process is lifelong, complex, beautiful, agonizingly (at times) grandiose and difficult, (to put a little flesh on the bare bones) humiliating, uglifying, stereotypifying, grim, ordinary, and probably worth the pitched battle which it often is. Certainly, in Stephen we witness much of the process which may be even more marked with Leopold. But ordering for Stephen in *A Portrait* is also related to his scholarship, his ability with words. One of his greatest pleasures is to treat his family with his scholarship prize winnings, certainly an indication of giving back to the community, namely his family, which had supported him. His chaos seems diminished in fits and starts.

As for Leopold Bloom of *Ulysses*, he seems to have literally lost touch and communication with Molly after Rudy's death. His ten-year Kaddish for Rudy is an indicator of his loss and seemingly lost soul. His incredible involvement with mourning becomes both his hubris and his sorrow. He figuratively feels castrated and is literally impotent. However, as with Prometheus and perhaps other gods before him, Bloom's impotence is textually both temporary and symbolic.

Molly is involved with the loss, not so completely with Rudy, but with Leopold. She felt the necessity to take a lover for herself because of his impotence. But it was Rudy's death which led to the set of circumstances which existed between the two. Bloom is not completely crippled by the experience, but readers must follow him into his personal hell and catharsis, in his one day walk through Dublin. Odysseus had difficulty getting home from the Trojan War in a series of episodes and actions which ultimately left him quite alone, but not friendless. Like him, Bloom is never completely friendless, although his friendships are superficial. When he does connect with Stephen in Chapters 16 and 17 of the book, his gripping fantasies are on the wane or in the flux of change. Bloom's feelings are intact, but his timing has run amok and aground in a seemingly endless sense of timeless suspension of inertia and "going through the motions."

A reader's strongest impression of both Stephen and Leopold can be that they are inextricably linked through the dynamics of their personalities. Leopold needs someone to teach him, and Leopold can do that. Stephen seems to be linked to eternal youth, symbolically, and Leopold to the wisdom of the ages. In the father/son motif of the two, these two impulses seem fused symbolically and centrifugally.

While talking and thinking about the difference in ages between himself and Stephen, Bloom in "Ithaca" fantasizes himself to be annually, exponentially at varying factors, a great number of years older than Stephen. When Stephen reaches the age of Methuselah, or 969, Bloom will be 83,300 years old, having progressed in time and regressed (psychologically) simultaneously, which is one of the most profound themes of *Ulysses*: the backward-forward, seesawing aspect of time. In Bloom's fantasy he is linked with the gods of the early Greek period, and, therefore, before the written word and remembrance of language as we now experience it, in fact. The fantastic of his fantasy is also phenomenological. Greek religion has validity in the realm of the fantastic and within the philosophy of mind, whether or not one personalizes the symbols consciously. Symbolically, Bloom is linked to Odysseus, to the patriarchs, to Christ, and then importantly to the Zeus-Prometheus-Epimetheus-Fire paradigm through his special suffering and his need to share his matches, candles, and fires with Stephen. Bloom felt himself to be a teacher, a teacher of Gentiles; but he also showed the "light" to Gentiles. Although Bloom, in talking with Stephen, dissented tacitly from Stephen's views on the eternal affirmation of the spirit of man in literature (Joyce, 1961, 665), Bloom was part of that affirmation of the spirit of man whether he agreed or not. James Joyce made him of such stuff.

One must view the myth of Prometheus as a myth of advocacy and the god Prometheus as an advocate, allegory, analogy to, and metaphor of one aspect of the spirit of man/woman—and in that sense a teacher of the needs and ways of individuals to themselves concerning the necessities of life, including fire in its positive allegorical aspects. James Joyce used the Promethean allegory in a modern minimalist form for one chapter of *Stephen Hero*, rewrote it for *A Portrait*, and included it in *Ulysses*.

Bloom was crippled like Prometheus, but not beaten, also like Prometheus. What can be most significant to one as a reader of Ulysses is the poignancy of Bloom's dilemma. To be without his child as an heir was a tragedy, as it often has been for families historically. The classic tragedy for Leopold Bloom was not only that Rudy died, but that Leopold mourned, and mourned, and mourned when he could have tried again for other sons. James Joyce, with the linkage of Stephen and Leopold, leaves us with the speculative symbolic possibility that Leopold will try again for other sons, because of his surrogate relationship to Stephen as son, and Stephen's reciprocation of this affection and concern.

Too, Bloom lit a fire for Stephen in *Ulysses*. Stephen was as a nettle in Bloom's side, forever green, forever young, forever vulnerable. And Stephen, too, lit a fire for Bloom, but in Bloom's mind it was sparked, without matches, but matched with Bloom's love. In so doing, he pays homage to Bloom. He shared his knowledge; they shared their knowledge. It was the pleasure of their company together which seemed to keep them fused together, inexplicably intertwined. It was both their self love and self malice which helped them when they were together, their malice honed with love. Both seem Promethean, coming into their own, with self knowledge and community as powerfully motivating forces.

But to begin in the beginning with Joyce's text *Stephen Hero*, before one can fully come to understand Bloom and Stephen together, a discourse occurs between Father Butt and Stephen Hero concerning lighting a fire. It is termed "a useful art" and, for all we know, this fire-lighting of which Father Butt spoke may partake or imply something of the paradoxical finite/infinite quality of useful arts and of life itself. A *New York Times* article in the February 23,1982, Science Section, discussed life's origin. Dr. Cyril Ponnamperuma is "at the forefront of research into life's origins".

A theory proposed by others and built upon by Dr. Ponnamperuma is that lightning started it all. (Wilford)

Father Butt and Stephen in their aggrandizement of the act or function of building a fire (no lightning here, for the moment, except for the lightning of recognition) and relating this act to the realm of the artistic have changed the act to an aesthetic. The fire has become allegorical, metaphoric, somewhat personified in its connectedness to the artist, and hence, anthropomorphized, if ever so slightly. There is nothing purely psychological about how fire has become so used and transformed. Building a fire is a physical act. Making fire into a "useful art" is philosophical and the presumption of a literary aesthetic; and as part of a cognitive function or action—it is very physical. James Joyce has herein extended the Promethean allegory while keeping some of the original elements of Hesiod extant, with others transformed, and yet others metamorphosized to a degree. In his transformation of the narrative, which is done on a *microcosmic* scale and then extended into the theme, Joyce is reifying his understanding of "the eternal affirmation of the spirit of man in literature." His style, arduous at times, is especially a challenge here.

Within Chapter I of *Stephen Hero* there are three strong verbal parries. They occur between Stephen Hero and Father Butt, as expostulated above. There are circumlocutions and circumspections within the mind of the heroic Stephen, which the reader must note. Other characters appear, but Father Butt and Stephen in their discourse stand out as being primary within this chapter. Their circumambulation and dialogues all underscore their obvious differences and characters, as well as their modes and styles of interacting within their environments. Readers then try to circumscribe their meanings, to the best of our, what one hopes will be, indefatigable spirits.

Father Butt was one of the "visible lieutenants" of the President of Belvadere College. He was dean of the college and professor of English. Stephen did not really like him. He found Father Butt's reading of verse to be the worst. Also, Father Butt was always covered with chalk, which gave him a dry look, or a burned, ash-like look. His raspy voice even sounded dry. We are not surprised then to learn that he spoke to a Total Abstinence Club, certainly a dry group in one sense. He was trying to convince the membership that Shakespeare was a Roman Catholic, with what clear motive we cannot guess. But James Joyce was fond of conversions, too, but of a different sort. Father Butt was the butt of one of Joyce's internal jokes within this chapter.

Isaac Butt, whom the character of Father Butt is based upon, was the founder of the Irish Home Rule Party which entered Parliament in 1874. Butt was from a "body of fairly prosperous Irish gentlemen". In 1877, there was a split in the Home Rule Party in which Charles Stewart Parnell and Isaac Butt found themselves on opposite sides. In that same year, Parnell replaced Butt as the Chairman of the Home Rule Confederacy in Ireland. Butt would die two years later. Parnell during this period, and for about the next twelve years, enjoyed a great popularity. His involvement with and for land agitation, and his obstructions within Parliament, had contributed to the disfavor of Butt, the more conservative figure.

Joyce places Stephen and Father Butt in opposition within this chapter, much as Isaac Butt and Charles Parnell, both Irish Catholics, were in opposition—by, in, and with matters of degree. Stephen shall not suffer the fate of a Parnell, not completely, although he was such a maverick and free spirit as Parnell was.

With his affirming interest in poetics, Stephen believed that poetry should be read according to its stresses as they occurred in rhyme. Father Butt believed poetry should just be read, on the other hand. At one point, he did agree with Stephen's theory, as much as Father Butt could agree with anything. Stephen, among his other admirable traits, loved words. He was appalled to sense the shallowness with which words were used by most people:

> And pace by pace as this indignity of life forced itself upon him, he became enamoured of an idealism, a more veritable human tradition. (Joyce 1963, 26)

Father Butt, on the other hand, could institutionalize everything including the value of language. Stephen could corporealize ideas in opposition, and fine dialectical form, a dangerous habit to institutions, at times. When Father Butt encouraged Stephen to write for newspapers, the reader is prepared to find the idea repugnant to Stephen because of his love for words—beyond the kind of involvement with words that journalists may presumably have.

In their first parry, Butt was admiring of Stephen's compositions. To Stephen, acknowledging his interest in the literary:

> Words, he said, have a certain value in the literary tradition and a certain value in the market-place—a debased value. (1963, 28)

Joyce, later in *Ulysses*, in the "Aeolus" chapter, placed Stephen within the midst of the traffic of newspaper headlines. There all of these market-place words, with their debased value, are used with great effect and hilarity. Joyce has that ability to transform the low-down, by incorporating it into his literature as part of his expression and understanding of teleos. Stephen, therein, fit well under the head of OMNIUM GATHERUM.

Stephen began to be taken seriously, though, by Butt when Stephen stated that he hoped that he was not detaining Butt by engaging him in conversation. Father Butt began to be circumspect about the word "detain" as if he were suddenly in custody or enthralled. He sped off at this point so that he might begin another parry with Stephen the next morning. The reader imagines Butt as a road-runner, a comic figure, and as one of Dante's infernal flagellates (internally flagellated here), rather obsessed, but this time by the whir of the word whip which was being either shared or imposed upon him by Stephen.

Father Butt, the next morning, in the apropos Physics Theatre (of Life, is one of the suggestions) is lighting "a small fire in a huge grate". Father Butt infers that he, himself, is an "artist" when he says, "There is an art to lighting a fire", which fire in said grate he had actually started or begun with three dirty candle-butts, another play on Butt's character. He seems himself like a candle-butt, in imagination, stubby and easy to flare. But the candle butts were withdrawn from Father Butt's chalky soutane. It is clear that Joyce's two small paragraphs with three sentences of dialogue are packed with innuendo, dramatic irony and catalogue information. Father Butt, Roman Catholic, here replaces the "pagan" god Zeus; the traditions of power and institution have changed hands completely from Greek to Roman minatory, in Stephen's mind, authority. The analogies have not been lost, however, through syncretism and assimilation. The candles are representative of one of the many icons of the Roman Catholic Church, symbols of bringing light to the world, the light of salvation through the Trinity. This candle (with its ignitable wick within the wax) surely is not that different from the fennel-stalk, wherein Prometheus hid fire, to bring to personkind. Stephen, though, upon hearing Butt's remark that

There is an art, Mr. Dedalus, in lighting a fire.

states:

> So I see, sir. A very useful art. (1963, 28)

Joyce gives this second statement to Butt in *A Portrait*. But here Butt replies:

> That's it: a useful art. We have the useful arts and we have the liberal arts. (1963, 29)

This is a very contradictory statement. For Butt has first stated or implied the connection of art and fire metaphorically, and religiously (or iconographically), but states that wisdom of symbols for him cannot extend into literature. Ironically, the liberal arts for Butt are a fulcrum for his religiosity, a vehicle for the expression of his Catholicism, be it ever so shallow. They are not only philosophically useful, per se, but functional for him.

Stephen uses Butt's shallowness in very interesting ways. He resists it because his artistic sensibility leads him into a new aesthetic, and into an asceticism which incorporates the shallow elements, transforming them, while at the same time infusing them with energy, much as Butt lights the candle analogously. This energy seems so absent in Butt's mouth, in his statements, because the reader senses that he is trying to control Stephen somehow, whether or not he is conscious of this. However, he, too, is trying to share with Stephen, in spite of their different values. Then Joyce describes Stephen, in his uniqueness, intrapsychically beyond the conversation with Butt:

> It was not only in Skeat that he found words for his treasure-house, he found them also at haphazard in the shops, on advertisements, in the mouths of the plodding public. He kept repeating them to himself till they lost all instantaneous meaning for him and became wonderful vocables. (1963, 30)

Butt as a symbolic stand-in for the minimilized, symbolic Zeus (conflated from his Greek pantheon and sky into the corpus of human nature) had provided an antithetical statement, or metaphor, for the symbolic

Promethean Stephen, the artistic seeing being. Within his artistry is a definition of his being. He is attempting to go beyond one level of experience to another, but Butt keeps on being Butt, representing a more status quo stance than Stephen could experience. Within Butt's thought, there is not the ability to go beyond a specific literal level because his thought appears to have a certain, limited dimensionality or differentiality.

Within Aeschylus, we were shown Zeus and Prometheus at odds: Prometheus must be punished, one remembers, for his expression of independence in giving humans fire which was to provide a liberation for their benefit, in more than one way. Prometheus wanted freedom from this punishment, and that freedom ultimately occurred. He and his kind of thought are immortal just as Joyce's "eternal affirmation" is suggestive within Stephen's relationship with Bloom, for one, of immortality—a symbolic, familial bond.

Butt, on the other hand, wanted Stephen to write newspaper articles. To do so would be a punishment to Stephen's artistic sensibility, to his artistic or poetic drive, as he experiences it. What is useful to Butt is what keeps him in his functional place as priest, teacher, and administrator, but there is an art to lighting a fire which he cannot know. He cannot make connections between ideas. For Butt, the clown of *Twelfth Night*, for instance, sang songs to nobility because:

> It was a custom at that time for noblemen to have clowns to sing to them . . . for amusement. (1963, 29)

But part of the function of the clown in *Twelfth Night* is to encourage the nobility to see their foolishness: just how foolish everyone is, including the clown. Butt, however, took *Othello* more seriously in a classroom discussion; but Stephen noted at the end of his discourse that the President of the College had refused to let two students see the play because of the "many coarse expressions in the play." Stephen's revenge, or freedom from the limitations of defining words ultimately is to not be a fool to himself, but to allow himself to fool with words, to be amused and to make powerful combinations with his word puzzles. To do this he needed silence:

> Phrases came to him asking to have themselves ex-
> plained . . . In class, in the hushed library, in the
> company of other students he would suddenly hear a
> command to begone, to be alone, a voice agitating the
> very tympanus of his ear, a flame leaping into cere-
> bral life. (1963, 30)

Thus, the flame is the cognitive spark for Stephen as he made what was for him the maximum use of his full thoughts. His thoughts burned for expression, from fire-place, to mind, to world.

In Joyce's rewrite of the fireplace scene in *A Portrait*, Father Butt is transformed into a very self-assured, nameless dean. His namelessness, like that of Victor Frankenstein, II, marks him out in a very fascinating way; he is an elemental chaotic figure. He does not appear limited or hollow, immediately, although Stephen describes him as so. The dean does not run away; he stokes his fire rather diabolically (as much as Zeus might have thrown his thunderbolt or seduced Olympian and earthly women) that it might have more abundant "life." The fire was made with coal and paper and lit this time with four candle butts. The dean seems completely arid, much like Melville's Ahab. Stephen notes that the dean:

> had remained ungraced by ought of saintly or prelatic
> beauty . . . his very soul had waxed old in that ser-
> vice without growing towards light and beauty . . .
> (Joyce 1967, 185)

Zeus, too, in denying humans fire, lacked the ability to share light of various sorts, and had limited overall vision. The implication is, however, for the dean (from his firebuilding), he could light a fine fire. Their dialogue here is clearly defined, more direct and candid, less halting than in *Stephen Hero*. It seems also less emotional and more clipped. Stephen, humbly, and rather dumbly, states that he is sure that he "could not light a fire". The dean then unflinchingly states, and perhaps generously:

> You are an artist are you not, Mr. Dedalus? . . . the
> object of the artist is the creation of the beautiful.
> What the beautiful is, is another question. (1967, 185)

Stephen then quotes Aquinas on the beautiful. Fire is
beautiful because it is pleasant to look at, and because
it warms the body it is good. "In hell, however, it is an
evil." With that binary opposition in the conversation, the
dean added a draught, to heighten the flame of the fire.
Stephen did not see him as an evil person, but rather as
a functional person "like a staff in an old man's hand."
Does Stephen here represent the old man's hand? Stephen
does seem the elder of the two psychically, but the use-
fulness theme is retained by Joyce and stated rather
strongly within this analogy. The nameless dean does not
have the kind of love which Stephen has, but he does
still have a function, or place.

The nameless dean also has the aspect, at times, of
being menacing. He is precise and to the point, knowing
his steps and plays much as a fencer might. His quick
deftness would almost seem a personification and allegory of Zeus' aegis. He seems hell-bent, too, on being
able to get Stephen to define his aesthetic position, and
as the fire has receded into the background, we are prepared to receive new information. The metaphor of mental light emerges. Stephen states:

> . . . there is no such thing as free thinking inasmuch
> as all thinking must be bound by its own laws. (1967,
> 187)

This statement indicates that thought has a priori aspects; it also indicates a personification of thought. Ha!
retorts the dean. But Stephen is undaunted; he continues to talk with the priest:

> For my purpose I can work on at present by the light
> of one or two ideas of Aristotle and Aquinas. (1967,
> 187)

But Stephen quickly turns the metaphor of the light again
into the corporeal lamp. In so doing, he is a perfect foil

or match for the priest. And while both men are being perfectly polite to one another, their courtesy seems to hinge on metaphoric massacre. The priest's face to Stephen seemed "like an unlit lamp or a reflector hung in a false focus". The priest as the substitute and symbolic Zeus then tells the anecdote of Epictetus who had his lamp stolen from the base of a god idol. He then passes into the question of how to fuel a lamp, and discusses the fueling of the lamp through a funnel. All of this narrative talk is a replay of Prometheus' "stealing" of fire from Olympus in a fennel leaf.

At this point textually, Joyce adds a new twist to his narrative to bring his own historic moments into the syncretic play as he moves ideational from Greek to modern thought and structure. The priest/dean is made non Irish or English here, which would make him symbolically Parnell's enemy, and rather arch-fiend symbolically on one level for Stephen. The priest suggests that the differences between the beautiful and the sublime, between moral beauty and material beauty, must be speculated upon. But it would be inane for Stephen to so speculate, suggests the priest, because Stephen must concentrate upon getting his degree first; he must first graduate from school before he can delve and think about such differences. The liberal arts it would seem are, thus, for the priest meant to be useful arts, but not insightful ones. One may become insightful after the rite of passage has occurred.

But, another interesting change occurs in the narrative rewrite, which the reader must note carefully. Stephen has pity much as Percy Shelley's Prometheus has for Zeus, but here for the priest:

> A desolating pity began to fall like a dew upon his
> easily embittered heart for this faithful servingman of
> the knightly Loyola . . . (1967, 190)

And though Stephen in *Stephen Hero*:

> spent nights and days hammering noisily as he built
> a house of silence for himself wherein he might await
> his Eucharist, days and nights gathering the first
> fruits and every peace-offering and heaping them upon

his altar whereon he prayed clamorously the burning
token of satisfaction might descend. (1963, 30)

In one splitting moment of emotion (because of his pity
for the nameless dean in the *Portrait*), Stephen was freed
from his loneness and his spectral house of silence. That
pity was a corporeal Eucharist with spiritual ramifications. Finally, Stephen (like Prometheus) was freed from
the need for revenge, and the positive aspects of the narcissism of his soul stopped drowning.

While the fireplace scene in *Ulysses* is changed,
though holding ties to both fireplace scenes of *Stephen
Hero* and *A Portrait*, it takes place in the chapter called
"Ithaca." There is a seeming scientism which dominates
"Ithaca." Symbolic, poetic language is replaced in most
instances with staccato, descriptive narrative. There is a
comradery, a closeness which exists between Stephen and
Bloom which is relieving and sane after the madness and
intrepid chaos of "Circe." The leveling out from surreal-
ism through "Eumaeus" to a crisp reality, with innumer-
able and modern inventories, stops one short with the
sheer seeming sanity of it all.

Just as when Odysseus came home to find
Telemachus, some housekeeping was in order; so, too,
in "Ithaca" with Stephen and Leopold, the housekeeping
seems to be mental with the seeming need to remove
cobwebs from the old/young brains. Stephen and Leopold
are both seeming Promethean when they arrive to
Leopold's house. Bloom is "keyless" there, just as
Prometheus was "impotent" or limited as he was tied to
his rock; Bloom "breaks" into his home by climbing
through a window. But here his overcoming of obstacles
is handled intrapsychically, as Hercules had become a
built-in function of his ideation. He seemed freed just as
Prometheus had been from limitations (only Bloom did it
himself). This is a portentous beginning, and later
Stephen and Leopold will observe themselves in progres-
sive time, their changes, and make self revelations. Zeus
is subsumed as archetype from the scene: no more revenge, no more dominating authority figure who cannot
appreciate the beauty of humankind, no more internal

metaphoric opposition to freedom unto natural laws—no more humans, cousins, or uncles being rejected. The Promethean aspect of mind dominates—forethought or foreknowledge. The question for the two men was:

> Was there one point on which their views were equal and negative? The influence of gaslight or electric light on the growth of adjoining paraheleotropic trees. (Joyce, 1961, 667)

A return to Joyce's "light" theme bears fruitful results here as light affects growth: the light of mechanical things, resulting from the harnessing of nature, and the light of the mind resulting from attempts to communicate. Bloom recalls other nocturnal jaunts with other friends which were intellectually stimulating as he and Stephen began to relax.

The first thing Bloom did after he got keyless into his home was to ignite (not from a fireplace in this instance)

> a lucifer match by friction, set free inflammable coal gas by turning on the ventcock, lit a high flame which, by regulating he reduced to quiescent candescence and lit finally a portable candle. (1961, 667)

Bloom walked with his candle in hand to his front door at 7 Eccles Street, no longer impotent it seems, to let Stephen into his home. "Did Stephen obey his sign? Yes." The lit candle has thus become a sign of warmth, potential love, and community as their comradely stance had already seemed to indicate.

Bloom, the moment that Stephen entered into his home, extinguished the candle, bent down on one knee, and began to organize, like the dean, in the Bloom household grate, a pyre for fire. As Bloom began to work (with his inventory of flammable objects, most notably crosslaid resin-tipped sticks, various colored papers and pieces of coal) Stephen began to reflect upon the many people in his life who had kindled fires for him "kneeling on one knee or two". He thought

. . . of Brother Michael
. . . of his father, Simon Dedalus

. . . of his godmother Miss Kate Morkan
. . . of his mother Mary
. . . of the dean of studies, Father Butt
. . . of his sister Dilly (Delia). (1961, 670)

The fifth mention of "the dean of studies, Father Butt"
links us to the other two books immediately.

Bloom had ignited a lucifer match indicating that
even Lucifer had been tamed herein, controlled and
brought to the diminutive. Too, as Stephen raised his
gaze from Bloom's fire, across the room he saw Molly's
hosiery hung to dry. One wooden peg held her hose at
the midpoint juncture to the line. This is another symbolic, hopeful sign for Stephen and for Bloom, through
Joyce, who allows this symbol. For Stephen in *Stephen
Hero*, the flame in his mind, in his silent sepulchre, was
linked to his ejaculations as he walked the streets of his
college town. Here, too, in "Ithaca" the fire is linked to
sensuality. Stephen might, speculatively, one day have
as companion a woman friend/lover/wife as Bloom had
once had, and still has possibility of, with Molly.

Joyce has brought us full circle from *Stephen Hero*
to *Ulysses* in this one illuminating moment. However,
what seems full circle is instead an historical line or progression through these scenes in his books, united intrinsically with symbols of a potentially infinite nature.
Bloom raised his eyes from the fire he had built, as
Stephen had raised his, but to the range, where he was
to boil water for a drink for Stephen as an act of hospi-
tality, one of the very most important themes of the
Odyssey. Zeus, as noted in the beginning of this book,
was the protector of the law of host and guest, which
herein has become an intrapsychic reality, and, in this
instance, Bloom is the host. Then, Bloom has the opportunity to think upon what has been the most singular
satisfaction for him:

> To have sustained no positive loss. To have brought
> positive gain to others. Light to the gentiles. (1961,
> 676)

Here light is transformed to Judaic law and Judeo-Christian Christ in Bloom's recollection and reverie.

Stephen and Leopold are elemental forces of the Prometheus project structurally and symbolically within the text. Zeus seems to have been leveled, or transformed like the impotent Satan of Dante's *Inferno*—his kind of mind control has been tamed, or subdued. Once the representational tyrant of stagnant power, linked with Prometheus by growth, he has been replaced by a more loving, flexible kind of mind. Neither Stephen nor Bloom swoons like Narcissus into a river mirror:

> What was Stephen's auditive sensation? He heard in a profound ancient male unfamiliar melody the accumulation of the past.

> What was Bloom's visual sensation?
> He saw in a quick young male familiar form the predestination of a future. (1961, 689)

Stephen and Bloom are inextricably intertwined, though both unique personalities, and fused by the spirit of humankind in literature, as both the spirit of Prometheus, allegorically, and the eyes of a matured Narcissus. James Joyce brought Prometheus from the Caucuses and aspects of Narcissus from a drowning pool to positive and stronger recognitions, straight into the human heart through his characterizations—into people more like ourselves.

BETWEEN THE SUBSTANCE
AND SHADOW OF TRUTH:
IN CONCLUSION

James Russell Lowell in America, whose influence reached England, in 1843, described part of the Promethean power, as he conceived it with help from his authorial ancestors, in what was another evocative re-creation of the Hesiod allegory in his poem "Prometheus." In a speech with Zeus, he had Prometheus say:

> Yes, I am still Prometheus, wiser grown
> By years of solitude, —that holds apart
> The past and future, giving the soul room
> To search into itself; —and long commune
> With this eternal silence; —more a god
> In my long suffering and strength to meet
> With equal front the direct shafts of fate,
> Then thou in they faint-hearted despotism,
> Girt with thy baby-toys of force and wrath. (Lowell
> 40-41)

Here there is no more indirect, ambivalent messages— just strong, straight talk. He continues:

> Yes, I am that Prometheus who brought down
> The light to man, which thou, in selfish fear,
> Hadst to thyself usurped, —by his sole right,
> For man had right to all save Tyranny—
> And which shall free him yet from thy frail throne.
> Tyrants are but the spawn of ignorance,
> Begotten by the slaves they trample on

> Who, could they win a glimmer of the light,
> And see that Tyranny is always weakness,
> Or Fear with its own bosom ill at ease,
> Would laugh away in scorn the sandwove chain
> Which their own blindness feigned for adamant. (40-41)

Lowell's Prometheus offers a glimmer of light to help humans understand tyranny and the ideology of the slave perpetrator.

> Wrong ever builds on quicksands, but the Right
> To the firm centre lays its moveless base.
> The tyrant trembles, if the air but stir
> The innocent ringlets of a child's free hair,
> And crouches, when the thought of some great spirit,
> Over men's hearts, as over standing corn,
> Rushes, and bends them to its own strong will.
> So shall some thought of mine yet circle earth. (40-41)

Prometheus continues to offer his solid sense of right and goodness—the will of foreknowledge belongs to humans.

> Men, when their death is on them, seem to stand
> On a precipitous crag that overhangs
> The abyss of doom, and in that depth to see,
> As in a glass, the features dim and vast
> Of things to come, the shadows as it seems.
> Of what have been. Death ever fronts the wise;
> Not fearfully, but with clear promises
> Of larger life, on whose broad vans upborne,
> Their outlook widens, and they see beyond
> The horizon of the Present and the Past,
> Even to the source and end of things. (40-41)

The source and end of things are united; humans have a chance of greater life at the time of mortal death, a larger view of things.

> Such am I now: immortal woe hath made
> My heart a seer, and my soul a judge
> Between the substance and the shadow of Truth.
> The sure supremeness of the Beautiful,
> By all the martyrdoms made doubly sure
> Of such as I am . . . (40-41)

Lowell, like Joyce after him, brought readers back to human nature, and to specific truths in his poem. Lowell felt that his version of this theme, written in poetic form, was "the longest and best poem I have ever written, and overrunning with true radicalism and antislavery" (Lowell 39). There are new political issues at hand; one being that as beginning environmentalists, since many of the issues related to the barbarity of slavery and its aftermath in most Western nations, save the many symbolic ones, have been met, some world leaders and many citizens are concerned with issues of saving nature and the best of human nature, as we look around us; we see what is left of both and want to save the best of both if only we can. We do not have to falter and become ideological "slaves" to negative technocrats who might care less about both. Intrapsychically and within society, one must be Promethean in the struggle for what is constructive and Herculean for the freedom to be so.

> And now bright Lucifer grows less and less,
> Into the heaven's blue quiet deep-withdrawn
> Sunless and starless all, the desert sky
> Arches above me, empty as this heart
> For ages hath been empty of all joy,
> Except to brood upon its silent hope,
> As o'er its hope of day the sky doth now. (39)

Lowell's interest was with the suffering and the cognitive awareness of "right" as a philosophy of remove from tyranny—and Zeus was his Lucifer, as his poem indicates. Lowell was a United States government figure who served as a diplomat to Madrid in 1877 and London in 1880. His political recognition of Prometheus was just as valid as other cultural renditions and aspects of the history of the allegory have been. Joyce then brought us to human compassion, beyond the suffering, with a strong interest in fire as a literal, figurative, and aesthetic element, if but briefly, in his texts.

Years earlier, in Act III, Scene IV, of Shelley's *Prometheus Unbound*, Earth spoke to Asia of other and already implied symbolic meanings for fire as love and sensuality:

> This is my torch-bearer,
> Who let his lamp out in old time with gazing
> On eyes from which he kindled it anew
> With love, which is as fire, sweet daughter mine,
> For such is that within thine own. (Zillman 175)

Lord George Gordon Byron, another important Romantic figure and friend of the Shelleys, had begun even earlier in 1806, at the age of eighteen, the first of three poems related to the Promethean theme (see *Lord Byron: The Complete Poetical Works, Vols. I-V* by Jerome J. McGann, ed.), reflecting an internal awareness of struggle between these symbolic cognitive figures Zeus and Prometheus. That first poem entitled "Fragments of School Exercises, From the Prometheus Vinctus of Aeschylus" has two verses extant, the first of which may be read in homage to Zeus and the second in homage to Prometheus as victim, and to his plight. In the second poem of 1814, Byron compares Prometheus and Napoleon in a poem entitled "[Prometheus and Napoleon]" and tries to do this by analogy to each of their falls, though with different ends to these falls. Prometheus' fate was "to give life" and Napoleon's "to desolate" life. Prometheus took flame from Heaven while Napoleon took flame from his "native hell." Byron's final poem of 1816 on this theme, although he does note Promethean impulses or sparks in *Manfred*, is entitled "Prometheus" and it is philosophically resonate for James Russell Lowell's poem of the same name. He composes in the third stanza of Prometheus:

> Thy Godlike crime was to be kind,
> To render with the precepts less
> The sum of human wretchedness,
> And strengthen Man with his own mind;
> . . .
> A mighty lesson we inherit:
> Thou art a symbol and a sign
> To Mortals of their fate and force:
> Like thee, Man is in part divine,
> A troubled stream from a pure source; (McGann IV, 32)

The projection of the gods into human form and vice-versa, from this ancient allegory, usually depicted or in-

dicated aspects of power issues beyond their usual recognition; they became grander because the allegory is part
of a cultural historical past in which humans are seen
as "winners" because of the protection of one god who
perceived feelings *other* than those of his own leader,
Zeus, who often played the role of the dictator: one who
had to be tamed and his thought made more flexible and
accepting. As earlier noted, the torch-bearer neglected his
fire but relit it by doing something completely "other;"
he gazed into someone's eyes with love and spontaneously his lamp, the figurative object, was relit and he
was re-energized to deal with lighting other literal and
figurative fires to help himself and others to be able to
see, or find a constructive way to clarity.

Love, a tremendous source of energy, is not beyond
scientific and biological laws as we know them; it is the
strongest basis of all cultural heritage, as studies of
mind/body medicine have so strongly revealed (e.g.,
psycho-neuro-immunology). Through the use of projected
ideas into and from the allegory of Hesiod, identity and
its complexity in both positive and negative forms for the
individual and society have been complexly related to
issues such as thought, social mores, the law, behavioral patterns, and to more instinctive issues and feelings such as anger, love, grief, pity, revenge, the giving
up of the need-for-revenge, sensuality, and rationality (to
name a few). Hesiod (as our guide [and his later imitators who used his name]) in his exhortations to his
brother Perses could never have dreamed or imagined the
complex expansions to which these exhortations would
lead.

The use of these ancient archetypes within works of
art, used either consciously or unconsciously, links readers to the past in shared emotion and shared potential
understanding; the varied uses and meanings within
Hesiod's paradigm, both literal and figurative, are with
us today and sometimes in ever more subtle forms. Robert Lowell re-bound Prometheus in his *Derived from
Aeschylus: Prometheus Bound* in 1967. His derivation is
not in poetic form but its dramatic prose is conversa-
tional (with some colorful colloquialisms used), philo-

sophical, psychological, and expressive of the difference between himself, his newly emerged postmodern era, and the language of Aeschylus and the Aeschylean world. Like Eric Alfred Havelock in 1951, in his translation of the *Prometheus Bound* of Aeschylus, there is some interpretation and concern for Prometheus as an intellectual being—and the difficulties for intellectual persons in existence in a seeming nonintellectual cosmos, including some of their personal concerns and fears expressed both directly and symbolically. Salman Rushdie's text *Grimus*, of 1975, is replete with characters with perverse psychological natures of one sort and another, or so it seems; but, nonetheless, he closely links Eastern and Western allegories and myths (including that of Prometheus) near the end of his text and transforms aspects of everyday life using aspects from the emerging paradigms of modern physics (the black hole, worm hole, or the Hawking radiation) metaphorically and allegorically, to create another reality which has many bizarre twists, capable of imploding, or gravitating to a chaotic end, which his *Grimus* does. The main character of *Grimus* finds an entryway to a new reality while at sea, in an area with the reputation like that of the Bermuda Triangle. He goes through a hole in time to discover a wholly other, and perhaps more fragile, existence.

One is linked to the past through the Zeus-Prometheus-Epimetheus-Fire allegory not only in a linear, cultural and literary historical fashion, but also through the use of an imaginary circle wherein any point of entry touching modernity and postmodernity implies touching the ancient past simultaneously. Synchronic time may at times seem to defy scientific knowledge, but several scholars grapple with this issue in critical theory and in the sciences. Perhaps there is genetic coding from the ancient past of which we may eventually be made aware such as speculated upon by Carl Jung in his text "Concerning the Collective Unconscious." In the meantime, these literary and scientific remnants and speculations present us with several forms of kinship to that past, ones which resonate over and over again with implied allegorical messages of our *undermeanings* and our *open secrets*, which we may yet learn to value more.

SOURCES CITED

INTRODUCTION

1. Fletcher, Angus. *Colors of the Mind: Conjectures on Thinking in Literature.* (Cambridge, Massachusetts, and London, England: Harvard University Press, 1991), p. 94.
2. Donald, Merlin. *Origins of the Modern Mind: Three Stages in the Evolution of Culture and Cognition.* (Cambridge and London: Harvard University Press, 1991), p. 268.

CHAPTER I

1. Fletcher, Angus. *Colors of the Mind: Conjectures on Thinking in Literature.* (Cambridge, Massachusetts, and London, England: Harvard University Press, 1991), p. 94.
2. Lloyd-Jones, Hugh. *The Justice of Zeus, Sather Classical Lectures, Vol. Forty-one.* (Berkeley, Los Angeles, London: University of California Press, 1971), p. 5.
3. Pucci, Pietro. *Hesiod and the Language of Poetry.* (Baltimore and London: The Johns Hopkins Press, 1977), pp. 45–50.
4. Ibid., pp. 45–50.
5. West, M. L. *Hesiod, Works and Days.* (London, New York: Oxford University Press, 1978), pp. 3–26.
6. Ibid., p. vii.
7. Wender, Dorothea. *Hesiod (Theogony, Works and Days) and Theognis [Elegies].* (London: Penguin, 1973), p. 15.
8. Athanassakis, Apostolos N. *Hesiod: Theogony, Works and Days, Shield.* (Baltimore and London: The Johns Hopkins University Press, 1983), p. 43.
9. Davies, Paul. *Superforce: The Search for a Grand Unified Theory of Nature.* (New York: Simon and Schuster, 1984), pp. 16, 138, 165–166, 195, 199, 201, 203–205, 221.

10. Pagels, Heinz. *Perfect Symmetry: The Search for the Beginning of Time.* (Britain: Penguin Books, 1992), pp. 340–342.

10. McDonald, Kim A. " 'Discovery of the Century' Brings Instant Celebrity." *Chronicle of Higher Education* 1 July 1992: A8–A1.

11. Evelyn–White, Hugh G., trans. *Hesiod, The Homeric Hymns and Homerica.* (Cambridge, Massachusetts: Harvard University Press, 1936), p 17.

12. Solmsen, Friedrich. *Hesiod and Aeschylus.* (Ithaca, New York: Cornell University Press, 1936), p. 25.

13. Dods, Marcus, trans. *St. Augustine, The City of God.* (New York and London: Oxford University Press, 1936), p. 23.

14. MacDonald, Francis, trans. *Plato, The Republic of Plato.* (New York and London: Oxford University Press, 1945), p. 73.

15. Ibid., p. 73.

16. Robinson, John Mansley. *An Introduction to Early Greek Philosophy.* (Boston: Houghton Mifflin and Co., Inc., 1973), p. 27.

17. Ibid., p. 28.

18. Frick, Charlotte Ann. "The Zeus/Prometheus Paradigm in Selected Works." (New York: City College Master's Thesis [Reserve Section] Library), p. 8.

19. Blumenberg, Hans. *Work on Myth.* (Cambridge: MIT Press, 1987), p. 151.

20. Ibid., p. 151.

CHAPTER II

1. Ibid., vii–viii.

2. Bachelard, Gaston. *La Psychoanalyse du Feu.* (Paris: Gaalimard, 1945), p. 19.

3. Ibid., p. 27.

4. Murray, Gilbert; Rogers, Benjamin Bickley; Whitelaw, Robert, and others, trans. *Fifteen Greek Plays.* (New York: Oxford University Press, 1974), p. 14.

5. Donoghue, Denis. *Thieves of Fire.* (New York: Oxford University Press, 1974), p. 34.

6. Grimaldi, Alfonsina Albini. *The Universal Humanity of Giambattista Vico.* (New York: S. F. Vanni, Publishers and Booksellers, 1958), p. 96.

7. Scully, James; and Herington, C. J. *Aeschylus: Prometheus Bound.* (Oxford University Press: New York and London, 1975), p. 67.

8. Pagels, Heinz. *The Cosmic Code: Quantum Physics As The Language of Nature.* (Britain: Penguin Books, 1984), pp. 78–109 and 295.

9. Chopra, Deepak, M.D. *Quantum Healing: Exploring the*

Frontiers of Mind/Body Medicine (Bantam Books: New York, Toronto, London, Sydney, Auckland, 1989), pp. 107 and 217.

CHAPTER III

1. Evelyn–White. *Hesiod, The Homeric Hymns and Homerica.* pp. 79–80.
2. Burn, Robert. *The World of Hesiod, A Study of the Greek Middle Ages, c. 900–700, b. c.* (New York: E. P. Dutton and Co., 1937).
3. Op. Cit., p. 125.
4. Grimaldi. *The Universal Humanity of Giambattista Vico*, p. 96.
5. Op. Cit., p. 17.
6. Ibid., pp. 5–6.
7. Scully, James and Herington, C. J., trans. *Aeschylus, Prometheus Bound.* (New York and London: Oxford University Press, 1975), pp. 99–110.
8. Taplin, Oliver. *The Stagecraft of Aeschylus, The Dramatic Use of Exits and Entrances in Greek Tragedy.* (London: Oxford, At the Clarendon Press, 1977), p. 240.
9. Spatz, Lois. *Aeschylus.* (Boston: Twayne Publishers, Twayne's World Author Series, 1982), p. 144.
10. Evelyn–White. *Hesiod, The Homeric Hymns*, p.145.
11. Scully and Herington. *Aeschylus, Prometheus Bound*, p. 72.
12. Ibid., pp. 38–39.

CHAPTER IV

1. Bennesen, Anna. *With Shelley in Italy.* (New York: McMahon, A. C. McClurg and Co., 1970), p. 109.
2. Duerksen, Roland A., ed. *Percy Bysshe Shelley, The Cenci.* (Indianapolis and New York: The Bobbs Merrill Co., 1970), p. 109.
3. King–Hele, Desmond. *Erasmus Darwin.* (New York: Charles Scribner's Sons, 1963), p. 68.
4. Ibid., p. 68.
5. Ibid. pp. 50–51.
6. Joseph, E. K., ed. *Mary Wolstonecraft Shelley, Frankenstein, or The Modern Prometheus.* (London, New York and Toronto: Oxford University Press, 1969), p. 221.
7. Ibid., p. 28.
8. Ibid., p. 17.
9. Ibid., p. 37.
10. Ibid., p. 41.
11. Ibid., p. 44.
12. Ibid., p. 52.

13. Ibid., p. 52.

14. Ibid., p. 53.

15. Ibid., p. 54

16. Ibid., p. 54.

17. Ibid., p. 55.

18. Ibid., p. 57.

19. Ibid., p. 58.

20. Ibid., p. 223.

21. Winstanley, L., ed. *Shelley's Defence of Poetry and Browning's Essay on Shelley.* (Boston and London: D. C. Heath & Co., 1911) pp. 18–19.

CHAPTER V

1. Zillman, Lawrence John. *Shelley's Prometheus Unbound: The Text and the Drafts, Toward a Modern Definitive Edition.* (New Haven and London: Yale University Press, 1968), p. 43.

2. Ibid., p. 35

3. Ibid., p. 37.

4. Ibid., p. 41.

5. Winstanley, L., ed. *Shelley's Defence of Poetry and Browning's Essay on Shelley.* pp. 6–7.

6. Op. Cit., p. 37.

7. Grabo, Carl. *Prometheus Unbound, An Interpretation.* (New York: Gordian Press, 1968), p. 10.

8. Wright, John W. *Shelley's Myth of Metaphor.* (Athens: University of Georgia Press, 1968), p. 9.

9. Zillman, *Shelley's Prometheus Unbound,* p. 62.

10. Ibid., p. 67.

11. Ibid., p. 69.

12. Ibid., p. 67.

13. Young, Art. *Shelley and Nonviolence.* (Paris: Mouton, The Hague, 1975), p. 97.

14. Op. Cit., p. 67.

15. Ibid., p. 63.

16. Op. Cit., p. 159.

17. Hutchison, Thomas, ed. *Shelley Poetical Works.* (New York, London and Toronto: Oxford University Press, 1905), p. 39.

18. Ibid., pp. 78–79.

19. Ibid., p. 40.

20. Ibid., p. 40.

21. Zillman, *Shelley's Prometheus Unbound.* p. 77.

22. Ibid., p. 135.

23. Ibid., p. 159.

24. Ibid., p. 233.

25. Op. Cit., p. 193.

26. Ibid., pp. 441–442.

CHAPTER VI

1. Fabian, Bernhard: Mertner, Edgar; Schneider, Karl; Spevak, Marvin, eds. *Charles Kingsley, The Works.* (Hildesheim: George Olms Verlagsbuchandlung, Vol. II, 1969), p. 287.
2. McDonald, Kim. "Growing Body of Evidence Indicates Life Began in a Chemical Process Common in the Universe." *Chronicle of Higher Education* 8 Oct. 1986: 6–9.
3. Colloms, Brenda. *Victorian Visionaries.* (London: Constable, 1982), p. 2.
4. Huxley, Elspeth. *The Kingsleys, A Biographical Anthology.* (London: George Allen and Unwin, Ltd. Ruskin House, 1973), p. 264.
5. Ibid., p. 264.
6. Ibid., pp. 265–66.
7. Ibid., pp. 270–71.
8. Uffelman, Larry. *Charles Kingsley.* (Boston: G. K. Hall & Co., 1979), p. 71.
9. Fabian, Mertner, Schneider, Spevak, eds. *Charles Kingsley, The Works, Vol IX.* p. 385.

CHAPTER VII

1. Dobree, Bonamy (Gen. Ed.). *Bibliographic, Series of Supplements to British Book News on Writers and Their Work.* (London), Volume: *Robert Bridges* by John Sparrow, p. 7.
2. Ibid., p. 17.
3. Sparrow, John. *Robert Bridges Poetry and Prose with Appreciations by G. M. Hopkins, Coventry Patmore, Lionel Johnson, Laurence Binyon, and Others.* (Oxford: Clarendon Press, 1955), pp. 1–44.
4. Op. Cit., p. 31.
5. Ibid., p. 19.
6. Bridges, Robert. *Poetical Works of Robert Bridges.* (London, New York, Toronto, Melbourne, Bombay: Oxford University Press, 1914), p. 264.
7. Sparrow. *Robert Bridges Poetry and Prose.* Unnumbered Series. (London: Longmans, Green, 1962), pp. 1–44.
8. Bridges, Robert *Prometheus the Firegiver.* (Oxford. Private Press of H. Daniel, Fellow of Worcester College, 1883), pp. 1–70.

CHAPTER VIII

1. Sitney, P. Adams. *Modernist Montage: The Obscurity of Vision In Cinema and Literature.* (New York: Columbia University Press, 1991), p. 2.
2. Joyce, James. *Ulysses.* (New York: Vintage Books, 1961), p. 665.

3. Wilford, John Noble. "Life's Origin: A Scientist's Search for the Very Beginning." Science Times. *The New York Times*: 1982.

4. Joyce, James. *Stephen Hero*. (New York: New Directions, 1963), p. 26.

5. Ibid., p. 28.

6. Ibid., p. 28.

7. Ibid., p. 29.

8. Ibid., p. 30.

9. Ibid., p. 29.

10. Ibid., p. 30.

11. Joyce, James. *A Portrait of the Artist as a Young Man*. (New York: Viking Press, 1967), p. 185.

12. Ibid., p. 185.

13. Ibid., p. 187.

14. Ibid., p. 187.

15. Ibid., p. 190.

16. Joyce. *Stephen Hero*. p. 30.

17. Joyce. *Ulysses*. p. 667.

18. Ibid., p. 667.

19. Ibid., p. 670.

20. Ibid., p. 676.

21. Ibid., p. 689.

22. Ibid., p. 689.

23. Zillman. *Shelley's Prometheus Unbound*. p. 175.

CHAPTER IX

1. Scudder, Horace E., ed. *The Complete Poetical Works of James Russell Lowell*. (Cambridge, Massachusetts: The Riverside Press, 1968), pp. 39–41.

2. Ibid., p. 39.

3. Ibid., p. 39.

4. McGann, Jerome, ed. *The Complete Poetical Works of George Gordon Byron*. (Oxford University Press, 1980), Vol. IV, p. 32.

5. Zillman, Lawrence John. *Shelley's Prometheus Unbound: The Text and the Drafts, Toward a Modern Definitive Edition*. (New Haven and London: Yale University Press, 1968), p. 175.

BIBLIOGRAPHY

Abrams, M. H. *The Mirror and the Lamp: Romantic Theory and the Critical Tradition.* New York: W. W. Norton & Co., 1958.

Ahrmah, Ayi Kwei. *The Beautyful Ones Are Not Yet Born.* Boston: Houghton Mifflin, 1968.

Allen, Don Cameron. *Mysteriously Meant: The Rediscovery of Pagan Symbolism and Allegorical Interpretation in the Renaissance.* The Johns Hopkins Press: Baltimore and London, 1970.

Allen, F. D. trans. *N. Wecklein, The Prometheus Bound of Aeschylus and the Fragments of the Prometheus Unbound.* Boston and London: Gin and Co., 1891.

Appleman, Philip, ed. *Darwin: Texts, Backgrounds, Contemporary Opinion, Critical Essays.* New York & London: W. W. Norton & Company, 1979.

Athanassakis, Apostolos N. *Hesiod, Theogony, Works and Days, Shield.* Baltimore and London: The Johns Hopkins University Press, 1983.

Armstrong, Daniel and Van Schooneveld, C. M. *Roman Jakobson, Echoes of His Scholarship.* Lisse, The Netherlands: The Peter Pauper Press, 1977.

Bachelard, Gaston. *La Psychoanalyse du Feu.* Paris: Gaallimard, 1945.

141

Baker, Carlos. *Shelley's Major Poetry: The Fabric of a Vision*. New York: Russell and Russell, 1961 (c. 1948).

Baldick, Chris. *In Frankenstein's Shadow: Myth, Monstrosity, and Nineteenth-Century Writing*. Oxford: Clarendon Press, 1987.

Balfour, Graham. *The Life of Robert Louis Stevenson*. New York: Charles Scribner's & Sons, 1911 and 1915.

Beatty, Richmond Croom. *James Russell Lowell*. Hamden, Ct.: Archon Books, 1969.

Bennesen, Anna. *With Shelley in Italy*. New York: Charles Scribner's & Sons, 1905.

Bennett, Betty T., ed. *The Letters of Mary Wolstonecraft Shelley, Vols. I-III*.

Benson M. D., Herbert, and Proctor, William. *Beyond the Relaxation Response*. New York: Berkley Books, 1985.

Bibby, Cyril. *T. H. Huxley on Education*. Cambridge, England: Cambridge University Press, 1971.

Blessington, Marguerite (Power) Farmer Gardner. *Conversations of Lord Byron*. Ernest J. Lovell, Jr. ed. Princeton: Princeton University Press, 1969.

Bloomfield, Morton W., ed. *Allegory, Myth, and Symbol*. Samuel R. Levin's "*Allegorical Language*." Cambridge, Massachusetts and London, England: Harvard University Press, 1981.

Bloom, Harold. *Shelley's Mythmaking*. Cornell University Press: Ithaca, New York, 1969.

Bloom, Harold. *The Ringers in the Tower*. Chicago and London: The University of Chicago Press, 1971.

Bloom, Harold. *The Anxiety of Influence: A Theory of Poetry*. New York: Oxford University Press, 1973.

Blumenberg, Hans. *Work on Myth*. Trans. Robert Wallace. Cambridge, MIT Press, 1985 (c. 1979).

Blumenberg, Hans. *The Genesis of the Copernican World*. Trans. Robert Wallace. Cambridge: MIT Press, 1987 (c. 1975).

Blumenberg, Hans. *The Legitimacy of the Modern Age.* Trans. Robert Wallace. Cambridge: MIT Press, 1983 (c. 1966).

Borst, William Alvord. *Lord Byron's First Pilgrimage.* Hamden, Ct.: Archon Books, 1969.

Bowra, C. M. *Heroic Poetry.* New York: St. Martin's Press, 1966.

Bridges, Robert. *Prometheus, the Firegiver.* Oxford: Private Press of H. Daniel, Fellow of Worcester College, 1883.

Bridges, Robert. *The Shorter Poems of Robert Bridges.* London: George Bell and Sons, 1890.

Broad, William J. Broad. "A Voyage Into the Abyss: Gloom, Gold and Godzilla." *New York Times* 2 Nov. 1993: C1 & C12.

Browne, Malcolm. "Biologists Debate Man's Fishy Ancestors." *New York Times* 16 March, 1993: C1.

Browne, Malcolm. W. "Cave Find Shows Man and Apes Coexisting." *New York Times.* 11 January, 1994: C1 and C3.

Burn, Robert. *The World of Hesiod, A Study of the Greek Middle Ages c. 900-700 B.C.* New York: E. P. Dutton & Co., 1937.

Bush, Douglas. *Mythology and the Renaissance Tradition in English Poetry.* W. W. Norton & Co., Inc.: New York, 1963.

Butler, Eliza Marian. *Byron and Goethe: Analysis of a Passion.* London: Bowes and Bowes, 1956.

Capra, Fritjof. *The Tao of Physics: An Exploration of the Parallels Between Modern Physics and Eastern Mysticism.* Boston: Shambhala, 3rd ed., 1991.

Calvert, William Jonathan. *Byron: Romantic Paradox.* New York: Russell and Russell, 1962 (c. 1935).

Cameron, Kenneth Neil. *Shelley and His Circle, 1773-1822,* Cambridge, Massachusetts, 1961.

Chadwick, H. M. *The Heroic Age*. Cambridge, England: Cambridge University Press, 1912 and 1967.

Chew, Samuel Claggett. *Byron in England: His Fame and Afterfame*. New York: Russell and Russell, 1965.

Chew, Samuel Claggett. *The Dramas of Lord Byron, A Critical Study*. New York: Russell and Russell, 1964.

Chitty, Susan. *The Beast and the Monk, A Life of Charles Kingsley*. New York: Mason/Charter, 1975.

Chitty, Susan. *Charles Kingsley's Landscapes*. London and Vancouver: David and Charles, 1976.

Chopra, M. D., Deepak. *Quantum Healing: Exploring the Frontiers of Mind/Body Medicine*. New York: Bantam Books, 1989.

Clarke, Isabel C. *Shelley and Byron, A Tragic Friendship*. London: Hutchison and Col, Ltd., 1934.

Cline, Clarence Lee. *Byron, Shelley, and Their Pisan Circle*. Cambridge: Harvard University Press, 1952.

Colloms, Brenda. *Charles Kingsley, The Lion of Eversley*. London: Constable, '1975.

Colloms, Brenda. *Victorian Visionaries*. London: Constable, 1982.

Cooke, Michael. *The Blind Man Traces the Circle: On the Patterns and Philosophy of Byron's Poetry*. Princeton, N. J.: Princeton University Press, 1969.

Cooper, Lane. *The Greek Genius and Its Influence: Select Essays and Extracts*. New Haven: Yale University Press, 1917.

Crawford, Michael. *Archaic and Classical Greece, A Selection of Ancient Sources in Translation*. Cambridge, New York: Cambridge University Press, 1983.

Crow, John A. *Greece: The Magic Spring*. Harper and Row: New York, Evanston, and London, 1970.

Culler, Jonathan D. *Structuralist Poetics, Structuralism, Linguistics, and the Study of Literature*. Ithaca, New York: Cornell University Press, 1975.

Davies, Paul. *God and the New Physics*. New York: Simon and Schuster, 1983.

Davies, Paul. *Superforce: The Search for a Grand Unified Theory of Nature*. New York: Simon and Schuster, 1984.

Dods, Marcus, trans. *St. Augustine, The City of God*. New York: The Modern Library, Random House, Inc., 1950.

Donald, Merlin. *Origins of the Modern Mind: Three Stages in the Evolution of Culture and Cognition*. Cambridge and London: Harvard University Press, 1991.

Donoghue, Denis. *Thieves of Fire*. New York: Oxford University Press, 1974.

Duberman, Martin B. *James Russell Lowell*. Boston, Houghton Mifflin, 1966.

Duerksen, Roland A., ed. *Percy Bysshe Shelley, The Cenci*. Indianapolis and New York: The Bobbs Merrill Co., 1970.

Dunn, Jane. *Moon in Eclipse: A Life of Mary Shelley*. New York: St. Martin's Press, 1978.

Elledge, W. Paul. *Byron and the Dynamics of Metaphor*. Nashville: Vanderbilt University Press, 1968.

Ellman, Richard. *James Joyce*. New York: Oxford University Press, 1974.

Epstein, Edmund. *The Ordeal of Stephen Dedalus*. Carbondale and Edwardsville: Southern Illinois University Press, 1971.

Evelyn-White, Hugh G. *Hesiod, the Homeric Hymns and Homerica*. Cambridge, Massachusetts: Harvard University Press, 1936.

Fabian, Bernhard; Mertner, Edgar; Schneider, K.; Spivek, Marvin, editors. *Charles Kingsley, The Works (1880-1885, Vol I-IX*. Hildesheim: George Olms Verlagsbuchhandlung, 1969.

Fairley, Barker, trans. *Goethe's Faust*. Toronto and Buffalo: University of Toronto Press, 1970.

Feldman, Burton and Richardson, Robert D. *Rise of Modern Mythology, 1680-1860*. Bloomington: Indiana University Press, 1972.

Feldman, Paula R., and Schott-Kilvert, Diana, eds. *The Journals of Mary Shelley, 1814-1844*. Oxford: At the Clarendon Press, 1987.

Feder, Lillian. *Ancient Myth in Modern Poetry*. Princeton: Princeton University Press, 1971.

Fletcher, Angus. *Colors of the Mind: Conjectures on Thinking in Literature*. Cambridge, Massachusetts and London, England: Harvard University Press, 1991.

Fletcher, Angus. *Allegory*. Ithaca: Cornell University Press, 1964.

Florescu, Radu R. *In Search of Frankenstein*. Boston: New York Geographical Society, Ltd., 1975.

Foley, John Miles, ed. *Oral Traditional Literature: A Festschrift for Albert Bates Lord*. Columbus, Ohio: Slavica Publishers, Inc., 1980.

Forry, Steven Earl. *Hideous Progenies: Dramatizations of "Frankenstein" From Mary Shelley to the Present*. Philadelphia: University of Pennsylvania Press, 1990.

Freud, Sigmund. *A General Introduction to Psychoanalysis*. New York: Liverright Publishing Co., 1972.

Freud, Sigmund. *Introductory Lectures on Psychoanalysis*. New York and London: W. W. Norton and Co., 1965.

Freud, Sigmund. *The Ego and the Id*. New York: W. W. Norton & Co., 1960.

Frick, Charlotte Ann. "The Zeus/Prometheus Paradigm in Selected Works, An Essay." Master's Thesis. New York: City College Reserve Library, 1985.

Gagarin, Michael. *Aeschylean Drama*. Berkeley, Los Angeles, London: University of California Press, 1962.

Gersen, Noel. *Daughter of Earth and Water*. New York: William Morrow and Co., 1973.

Gilbert, Sandra M., and Gubar Susan. *The Madwoman in the Attic, The Woman Writer and the Nineteenth Century Imagination*. New Haven and London: Yale University Press, 1979.

Gilbert, Murray; Bickley, Benjamin, Whitelaw, Robert, trans. *Fifteen Greek Plays*. New York: The Oxford University Press, 1943.

Gleick, James. *Chaos: Making A New Science*. New York, London: Penguin Group, 1987.

Godwin, William. *The Adventures of Caleb Williams or Things As They Are*. New York: Holt, Rhinehart and Winston, 1965.

Golden, Leon. *In Praise of Prometheus, Humanism and Rationalism in Aeschylean Thought*. Chapel Hill, North Carolina: The University of North Carolina Press, 1962.

Golfing, Francis, trans. *Frederich Nietzsche, The Birth of Tragedy and the Genealogy of Morals*. Garden City, New York: Doubleday, Inc., 1956.

Grabo, Carl. *The Magic Plant, The Growth of Shelley's Thought*. Chapel Hill, North Carolina: The University of North Carolina Press, 1936.

Grabo, Carl. *Shelley's Eccentricities*. New York: Gordian Press, 1968.

Greenslit, Ferris. *James Russell Lowell: His Life and Work*. Boston, Houghton Mifflin, 1905.

Grimaldi, Alfonsina Albini. *The Universal Humanity of Giambattista Vico*. S. F. Vanni, Publishers and Booksellers, 1958.

Hale, Edward Everett. *James Russell Lowell and His Friends*. Boston and New York: Houghton Mifflin and Co., 1901.

Harris, Styron. *Charles Kingsley, A Reference Guide*. Boston: G. K. Hall & Co., 1981.

Hartley, Allan John. *The Novels of Charles Kingsley, A Christian Social Interpretation*. England: The Hour Glass Press, 1977.

Hassan, Ihab Habib. *The Postmodern Turn: Essays in Postmodern Theory and Culture*. Columbus: The University of Ohio Press, 1987.

Havelock, Eric Alfred. *The Crucifixion of Intellectual Man (Incorporating a Fresh Translation into English Verse of the Prometheus Bound of Aeschylus)*. Boston: The Beacon Press, 1951.

Hawking, Stephen. *A Brief History of Time: From the Big Bang to Black Holes*. Toronto and New York: Bantam Books, 1988

Herington, C. J. *Aeschylus*. New Haven and London: Yale University Press, 1986.

Heymann, Clemens David. *American Aristocracy: The Lives and Times of James Russell, Amy, and Robert Lowell*. New York: Dodd, Mead, 1979.

Hine, Daryl, trans. *The Homeric Hymns and the Battle of the Frogs and Mice*. New York: Atheneum, 1972.

Hoffman, Frederick J. *The Mortal No: Death and the Modern Imagination*. Princeton, New Jersey: Princeton University Press, 1964.

Holenstein, Elmar. *Roman Jacobson's Approach to Languages, Phenomenological Structuralism*. Bloomington, Indiana: University of Indiana Press, 1976.

Holmes, Richard. *Shelley: The Pursuit*. Penguin Books: New York, London, 1987 (c1974).

Hotson, Leslie. *Shelley's Lost Letters To Harriet*. Faber & Faber Limited, 1930.

Howe, Irving. *Decline of the New*. New York: Harcourt, Brace & World, Inc., 1970.

Howe, Irving. *The Idea of the Modern in Literature and the Arts*. New York: Horizon Press, 1967.

Hurst, Michael. *Parnell and Irish Nationalism*. Toronto: University of Toronto, 1968.

Hutchison, Thomas, ed. *Shelley Poetical Works*. London and New York: Oxford University Press, 1905.

Huxley, Michael, ed. *The Root of Europe: Studies in the Diffusion of Greek Culture*. New York: Oxford University Press, 1952.

Huxley, Elspeth. *The Kingsleys, A Biographical Anthology.* London's George Allen and Unwin, Ltd. Ruskin House, 1973.

Innes, Mary M., trans. *Ovid, Metamorphoses.* Great Britain: Penguin Books, 1980.

Irvine, Wm. *Apes, Angels and Victorians: Darwin, Huxley and Evolution.* Cleveland and New York: The World Publishing Co., Meridian Books, 1959.

Jacobus, Lee, ed. *A World of Ideas.* New York: St. Martin's Press, 1986.

Jakobson, Roman. *Child Language, Aphasia, and Phonological Reversals.* The Hague and Paris: Mouton, 1968.

Jakobson, Roman. *Main Trends in the Sciences of Language.* London: George Allen and Unwin, Ltd. 1973.

Jakobson, Roman, and Waught, Linda R. *The Sound Shape of Language.* Berlin, New York, Amsterdam: Mouton de Gruyter, 1987.

Jakobson, Roman. *Language in Literature.* Cambridge, Massachusetts and London, England: The Belknap Press of Harvard University, 1987.

Jameson, Robert. *The Essential Frankenstein.* New York: Crescent Books, 1992.

Joseph, E. K., ed. *Mary Wolstonecraft Shelley, Frankenstein, or the Modern Prometheus.* London, New York and Toronto: Oxford University Press, 1969.

Joyce, James. *A Portrait of the Artist as a Young Man.* New York: The Viking Press, 1967.

Joyce, James. *Stephen Hero.* New York: New Directions, 1963.

Joyce, James. *Ulysses.* New York: Vintage Books, 1961.

Jones, Fred. L., ed. *Mary Shelley's Journal.* Norman: University of Oklahoma Press, 1947.

King-Hele, Desmond. *Erasmus Darwin.* New York: Charles Scribner's Sons, 1963.

Knight, George Wilson. *Lord Byron's Marriage: The Evidence of Asterisks*. London, Routledge and K. Paul, 1957.

Koszul, A., ed. *Proserpine & Midas: Two Unpublished Dramas by Mary Shelley*. London: Humphrey Milford, 1922.

Kuhn, Thomas S. *The Structure of Scientific Revolutions*. Chicago, London: The University of Chicago Press, 1969.

Kuhn, Thomas S. "The Essential Tension: Tradition and Innovation in Scientific Research." *A World of Ideas*. Lee Jacobus, ed. New York: St. Martin's Press, 1986.

Lacan, Jacques. *The Four Fundamental Concepts of Psychoanalysis*. New York: W. W. Norton and Co., 1978.

Lanse, Hal. W. "The Influence of Percy Bysshe Shelley on Mary Shelley's Frankenstein." Master's thesis. New York: Queen's College Reserve Library, 1991.

Leighton, Angela. *Shelley and the Sublime: An Interpretation of the Major Poems*. London: Cambridge University Press, 1984.

Levin, Samuel R. "Allegorical Language." *Allegory, Myth, and Symbol*. Morton Bloomfield, ed. Cambridge & London: Harvard University Press, 1981.

Levine, George and Knoepflmacher, U. C., eds. *The Endurance of Frankenstein, Essays on Mary Shelley's Novel*. California: University of California Press, 1979.

Lewis, Linda. *The Promethean Politics of Milton, Blake, and Shelley*. Columbia and London: University of Missouri Press, 1992.

Logan, James Venable. *The Poetry and Aesthetics of Erasmus Darwin*. Princeton: Princeton University Press, 1936.

Lloyd, Jones, Hugh. *The Justice of Zeus, Sather Classical Lectures, Vol. Forty-one*. Berkeley, Los Angeles, London: University of California Press, 1979.

Lowell, Robert. *Prometheus Bound, Derived from Aeschylus*. New York: Farrar, Strauss and Girous, 1967.

Lumbsden, Charles J. and Wilson, Edward O. *Promethean Fire: Reflections on the Origin of Mind*. Cambridge, Mass.: Harvard University Press, 1983.

MacDonald, Francis, trans. *Plato, The Republic of Plato*. New York and London: Oxford University Press, 1945.

McDonald, Kim. "*Growing Body of Evidence Indicates Life Began in a Chemical Process Common in the Universe*." *Chronicle of Higher Education*, 8 Oct. 1986: 6–9.

McGann, Jerome. *The Complete Poetical Works of George Gordon Byron, Vol I-V*. Oxford: Clarendon Press, 1980.

McGlinche, Claire. *James Russell Lowell*. New York: Twayne Publishers, 1967.

Marchand, Leslie Alexis. *Byron's Poetry: A Critical Introduction*. Boston, Houghton Mifflin, 1965.

Martin, Robert Bernard. *The Dust of Combat, A Life of Charles Kingsley*. London, England: Faber and Faber, 1959.

Medwin, Thomas. *Conversations of Lord Byron*. n Ed., Ernest J. Lovell, Jr. Princeton, New Jersey: Princeton University Press, 1966.

Mellor, Anne K. *Mary Shelley: Her Life, Her Fiction: Her Monsters*. Bloomington and Indianapolis: Indiana University Press, 1988.

Mellor, Anne K. *Romanticism and Feminism*. Bloomington and Indiana University Press, 1988.

Moore, Doris. *The Late Lord Byron: Posthumous Dramas*. Philadelphia: Lippincott, 1961.

Murray, Gilbert; Bickley, Benjamin; Whitelaw, Robert, (with others), trans. *Fifteen Greek Plays*. New York: The Oxford University Press, 1943.

Nemerov, Howard. *Figures of Thought, Speculations on the*

Meaning of Poetry and Other Essays. Boston: David R. Godine, 1978.

Nicolson, Harold George, Sir. *Byron, The Last Journey*. Hamden, Ct.: Archon Books, 1969.

Norris, Christopher. *Deconstruction, Theory and Practice*. London and New York: Metheun, 1982.

Notopoulos, James A. *The Platonism of Shelley, A Study of Platonism and the Poetic Mind*. Durham, North Carolina: Duke University Press, 1949.

Oates, Whitney J. & O'Neill, Jr. Eugene, eds. *The Complete Drama (All the Extant Tragedies of Aeschylus, Sophocles and Euripides, and the Comedies of Aristophanes and Menanger, In a Variety of Translations), Vol I*. New York: Random House, 1938.

O'Brien, Cruise. *Parnell and His Party, 1880-1890*. London: Oxford University Press, 1957.

Origo, Iris (Cutting), Marchesa. *The Lost Attachment: The Story of Byron and Tesersa Guiccioli*. New York, Scribner, 1949.

Pagels, Elaine. *Adam, Eve, and the Serpent*. New York: Vintage Books, 1988.

Pagels, Heinz R. *The Cosmic Code: Quantum Physics as the Language of Nature*. London & New York: Penguin Books, 1984.

Pagels, Heinz R. *Perfect Symmetry: The Search for the Beginning of Time*. Great Britain: Penguin Books, 1992.

Parker, Derek. *Byron and His World*. Viking Press, 1969. (c. 1968).

Pearson, Hasketch. *Dr. Darwin*. New York: Walker and Co., 1930.

Podlecki, Anthony J. *The Political Background of Aeschylean Tragedy*. Ann Arbor: The University of Michigan Press, 1966.

Pomorska, Krystyna, and Rudy, Stephen. *Roman Jakobson: Verbal Art, Verbal Sign, Verbal Time*. Basil Blackwell, 1985.

Priestley, F. E. L., ed. *William Godwin, Enquiry Concerning Political Justice and Its Influence on Morals and Happiness*. Toronto: The University of Toronto Press, 1946.

Prouty, Charles, ed. *William Shakespeare, Twelfth Night, or, What You Will*. Baltimore: Penguin Books, 1968.

Pucci, Peitro. *Hesiod and the Language of Poetry*. Baltimore and London: The Johns Hopkins University Press, 1977.

Quennel, Peter. *Byron in Italy*. New York: The Viking Press, 1941.

Quennel, Peter. *Byron, A Self Portrait: Letters and Diaries*. New York: Humanities Press, 1967.

Radin, Paul. *The Trickster: A Study in American Indian Mythology* (Commentaries by Karl Kereny and C. G. Jung). New York: Greenwood Press, 1969.

Rieger, James, ed. *Frankenstein: or, The Modern Prometheus, The 1818 Text*. Chicago and London: The University of Chicago Press, 1974, 1982.

Rieu, E. V., ed. *Homer, The Odyssey*. Great Britain: Penguin, 1979.

Reboul, Marc. *La Formation D'use Personalite et Son Affirmation Litteraire (1819-1850)*. Paris: Presses Universitaires de France, 1973.

Robinson, John Mansley. *An Introduction to Early Greek Philosophy*. Boston: Houghton Mifflin, 1968.

Ryan, Judith. *The Vanishing Subject: Early Psychology and Literary Modernism*. Chicago and London: The University of Chicago Press, 1991.

Sargent, Thelma, trans. *The Homeric Hymns, A Verse Translation*. New York: W. W. Norton and Co., Inc., 1973.

Scudder, Horace E., ed. *The Complete Poetical Works of James Russell Lowell*. Cambridge, Massachusetts: Houghton Mifflin, 1968.

Scully, James; and Herington, C. J. *Aeschylus: Prometheus Bound*. Oxford University Press: New York and London, 1975.

Seidel, Michael. *Epic Geography, James Joyce's Ulysses*. Princeton: Princeton University Press, 1976.

Siegel, Bernie. *Love, Medicine, and Miracles*. New York: Harper and Row, 1986.

Sitney, Adams P. *Modernist Montage: The Obscurity of Vision in Cinema and Literature*. New York: Columbia University Press, 1990.

Small, Christopher. *Mary Shelley's Frankenstein, Tracing the Myth*. Pittsburgh: University of Pittsburgh Press, 1973.

Smith, Herbert F., ed. *Literary Criticism of James Russell Lowell*. Lincoln: University of Nebraska Press, 1969.

Smoot, George and Davidson, Keay. *Wrinkles in Time*. New York: William Morrow and Company, Inc., 1993.

Solmsen, Friedrich. *Hesiod and Aeschylus*. Ithaca, New York: Cornell University Press, 1967.

Spark, Muriel. *Child of Light, A Reassessment of Mary Wolstonecraft Shelley*. Hadleigh, Essex, Great Britain: Tower Bridge Publications Limited, 1951.

Sparrow, John. *Robert Bridges Poetry and Prose with Appreciations* by G. M. Hopkins, Coventry Patmore, Lionel Johnson, Laurence *Binyon and Others*. Oxford: The Clarendon Press, 1955.

Sparrow, John. *Robert Bridges*. London: Bibliographic Series of Supplements to British Book News on Writers and Their Work. London: Longman, Greens, 1962.

Spatz, Lois. *Aeschylus*. Boston: Twayne Publishers, Twayne's World Author Series, 1982.

Stanford, William B. *Aeschylus, In His Style, A Study in Language and Personality*. Dublin: Dublin University Press, 1942.

Stevens, William K. "Want a Room With a View? Idea May Be in the Genes." *The New York Times* 30 Nov., 1993: C1.

Stevenson, Robert Louis. *Dr. Jekyll and Mr. Hyde, and Weir of Hermiston.* London, Edinburgh, Paris, Melbourne, Johannesburg, Toronto, and New York: Thomas Nelson and Sons, Ltd., 1956.

Stewart, Ian. *Does God Play Dice? The Mathematics of Chaos.* Oxford, Cambridge: Basil Blackwell, 1989.

Street, Brian V. *The Savage in Literature, Representation of the 'Primitive' Society in English Fiction (1858-1920).* London and Boston: Routledge and Kegan Paul, 1975.

Sunstein, Emily W. *Mary Shelley: Romance and Reality.* Boston: Little Brown and Co., 1989.

Taplin, Oliver. *The Stagecraft of Aeschylus, The Dramatic Use of Exits and Entrances in Greek Drama.* London: Oxford, At the Clarendon Press, 1977.

Thomson, George. *Aeschylus: The Prometheus Bound.* London: Cambridge at the University Press, 1932.

Thornburg, Mary K. Patterson. *The Monster in the Mirror: Gender and the Sentimental/Gothic Myth in Frankenstein.* Ann Arbor, Michigan: UMI Research Press, 1987.

Thorp, Margaret. *Charles Kingsley, 1819-1875.* New York: Octagon Books, 1969.

Trelawny, E. J. *Recollections of the Last Days of Shelley and Byron.* Boston: Ticknor and Fields, 1959.

Tropp, Martin. *Mary Shelley's Monster: The Story of Frankenstein.* Boston: Houghton Mifflin Company, 1977.

Uffelman, Larry. *Charles Kingsley, 1819–1875.* New York: Octagon Books, 1969.

Vance, Norman. *The Sinews of the Spirit, The Ideal of Manliness in Victorian Literature and Religious Thought.* Cambridge: Cambridge University Press, 1985.

Vasbinder, Samuel Holmes. *Scientific Attitudes in Mary Shelley's Frankenstein*. Ann Arbor, Michigan: UMI Research Press, 1976 and 1984.

Veeder, William. *Mary Shelley and Frankenstein: The Fate of Androgyny*. Chicago and London: The University of Chicago Press, 1986.

Wagenknecht, Edward Charles. *James Russell Lowell: Portrait of a Many-Sided Man*. New York: Oxford University Press, 1971.

Wasserman, Earl R. *Shelley's Prometheus Unbound: A Critical Reading*. Baltimore: The Johns Hopkins Press, 1965.

Weaver, Bennett. *Prometheus Unbound*. Michigan: University of Michigan, Archon Books, 1957 and 1969.

Welsford, Ened. *The Fool, His Social and Literary History*. Gloucester, Mass.: Peter Smith, 1968.

Wender, Dorothea. *Hesiod (Theogony, Works and Days) and Theognis (Elegies)*. London: Penguin, 1973.

West, M. L. *Hesiod, Works and Days*. London, New York: Oxford University Press, 1978.

Wilson, Edmund O. and Kellert, Stephen R. *The Biophilia Hypothesis*. Washington, D.C.: Island Press/Shearwater Books, 1993.

Wilford, John Noble. "Life's Origin: A Scientist's Search for the Very Beginning." *Science Times*. New York: *The New York Times*, 1982.

Winstanley, L., ed. *Shelley's Defence of Poetry and Browning's Essay on Shelley*. Boston and London: D. C. Heath and Co., 1911.

Wittreich, Joseph. *Visionary Poetics: Milton's Tradition and His Legacy*. San Marino, California: Henry E. Huntington Library and Art Gallery, 1979.

Wittreich, Joseph. *The Romantics on Milton: Formal Essays and Critical Asides*. Cleveland and London: The Press of Case Western Reserve University, 1970.

Woodhouse, A. S. P. *The Heavenly Muse: A Preface to Milton.* Toronto and Buffalo: University of Toronto Press, 1972.

Zillman, Lawrence John. *Shelley's Prometheus Unbound: The Text and the Drafts, Toward a Modern Definitive Edition.* New Haven and London: Yale University Press, 1968.

ABOUT THE AUTHOR

Charlotte Ann Frick is a published writer (essayist, journalist, poet, and screenwriter); a teacher (having taught at Queens College, Baruch College, and Rutgers University); a painter (with paintings in several private collections); an editor (formerly with several New York publishing houses); and a professional administrator (formerly with the Conservation of Human Resources project at Columbia University; the Museum of the American Indian {now the National Museum of the American Indian/Smithsonian} and presently with The Graduate School and University Center of the City University of New York). Educated in the United States (Columbia University and the City University of New York), and England (the University of London and Oxford University {Exeter College}), she holds two master's degrees (one in Creative Writing and one in English Language and Literature) and the Ph.D. in English Language and Literature (with a specialization in psychoanalytic theory) from Somerset University (with sites in the United States, England, and Belgium). In 1990, she was honored to receive a Woman of the Year award. For 1991–1992 she was named an International Woman of the Year and received a Woman of the Decade award in 1992. She resides happily in New York City.